Relapse Prevention for Sexual Harassers

Relapse Prevention for Sexual Harassers

Kirk A. Brunswig, M.S.
University of Nevada
Reno, Nevada

and

William O'Donohue, Ph.D.
Nicholas Cummings Professor of Organized Behavioral Healthcare Delivery
University of Nevada
Reno, Nevada

Springer Science+Business Media, LLC

ISBN 978-1-4613-5223-5 ISBN 978-1-4615-0749-9 (eBook)
DOI 10.1007/978-1-4615-0749-9

Originally published by Kluwer Academic/Plenum Publishers in 2002
Softcover reprint of the hardcover 1st edition 2002

10 9 8 7 6 5 4 3 2 1

A C.I.P. record for this book is available from the Library of Congress

Kirk thanks Mary Lee Sullivan Brunswig and Norman W. Brunswig
for demonstrating the value of education,
and Reo and Pike for their love and support through this process.

Bill thanks Jane Fisher, Katie O'Donohue, and Anna O'Donohue
for their continued love.

The authors extend their gratitude to Cathi D. Harris, M.A.,
Stephen C. Hayes, Ph.D., and Terri Rodman, Ed.D.,
for their comments on earlier drafts of this work.

Preface

This manual is intended as a stand-alone treatment manual. Useful background reading for this text is *Relapse Prevention with Sex Offenders* (Laws, 1989), and *Remaking Relapse Prevention with Sex Offenders: A sourcebook* (Laws, Hudson & Ward, 2000). The information contained in these books provides an adequate foundation for the foci, skills, and techniques presented in this manual.

There are several treatment targets for sexual harassers: analysis of, and coping with, high-risk situations; cognitive distortions and myth acceptance; denial and minimization; victim empathy; outcome expectancies; and deviant sexual fantasies, social skills, and lifestyle balance (Grundman et al., 1997). This treatment manual is written for therapists providing psychotherapy to sexual harassers in individual sessions, while human resources personnel and management staff may find this text a useful resource. The treatment is designed to be appropriate for male and female harassers, although because sexual harassment is a gendered problem, most clients will be males. The therapy sessions are intended to be sequential, that is, clients will not progress to the next module until they have mastered the content from their current module. It is expected that each module will take between two and four weeks to complete. While relapse prevention has been shown effective in both individual and group programs (Hall, 1995; Laws, 1989), this was written for individual treatment, but can be adapted for use with groups.

Contents

1

Introduction to Sexual Harassment
THE LAW AND CONSEQUENCES

DEFINITIONS AND MEASURES: WHAT IS SEXUAL HARASSMENT?

Fitzgerald, Swan and Magley (1997) discuss two major types of sexual harassment. First, *quid pro quo* harassment includes advancement, hiring or compensatory gain provisional on sexual interactions. It can also include demotion, firing or financial loss provisional on withholding of sexual interactions. The second and more common form of sexual harassment involves the creation of sexually hostile environment. Conte (1997) provides these examples of hostile environment harassment: offensive or explicit signs, calendars, literature, photographs, graffiti and verbal conduct. Thus, an offensive environment can be created by verbal or non-verbal behaviors.

Fitzgerald et al. (1997) further divide hostile environment harassment into two components: gender harassment and unwanted sexual attention. Gender harassment is not directed at sexual cooperation, but instead it is intended to demean, denigrate, or insult the victim, or a category of victims. For example, sexual epithets, gestures, slurs towards members of a gender, and pornographic material would fall under the heading of gender harassment. It is important to note that these misbehaviors may simply involve gender (e.g., "all women are dumb") and need not involve sexual or erotic content.

Unwanted sexual attention can include verbal and non-verbal behaviors (Fitzgerald et al., 1997). Whereas *quid pro quo* harassment involves the offer of an exchange of gain for sexual acts, unwanted sexual attention is the introduction of unwanted sexual requests without promises of benefits or an exchange of gain for sexual acts, unwanted sexual attention is the introduction of unwanted sexual requests without promises of benefits or withholding of punishment. Fitzgerald et al. (1997) combine gender harassment and unwanted sexual attention for behaviors legally considered hostile environment harassment, while naming *quid pro quo* harassment as sexual coercion.

Sexual harassment can also involve criminal sexual behaviors such as assault and even rape. Typically sexual harassment litigation is a civil action in which the victim is suing for redress of injuries. However, in certain cases the perpetrator may also be exposed to criminal prosecution.

It is important to note that the definitions of sexual harassment; what does and does not constitute sexual harassment can vary over the course of time and jurisdiction. However, what has not changed serves as a useful rule of thumb. What the courts have continued to endorse in the notion that sexual harassment is unwanted sexual behavior.

EFFECTS AND CONSEQUENCES

Sexual harassment impacts the victim, the harasser, and the organization. Whereas the direct costs of litigation and liability can be quantified quite easily, the effect on the organizational climate and workplace productivity as well as the psychological impact is not as easily assessed.

Dansky and Kilpatrick (1997) describe the effects of sexual harassment on the victim in terms of responses to sexual harassment, work-related effects, psychological effects, and physical or somatic effects. The most common victim response is to ignore, or attempt to ignore the harassment. When ignoring does not work, Dansky and Kilpatrick report that the victims will then tend to attempt to manage the harassment by redirecting conversations, avoiding the harasser, or even leaving the environment altogether (e.g., quitting the job, dropping the class, transferring schools). Examples of the explanations victims offer for indirect responses are self-blame for harasser's behavior, ignorance of remediatory options, severe consequences to harasser, and helplessness. These indirect attempts to address the harassment are often unsuccessful, and sometimes result in an escalation of the harassment (Rabinowitz, 1990). It should also be noted that in some minor cases, sexual harassment can have few or no major effects.

Although not discussed in the empirical literature, there are a few reports of the effects of sexual harassment on those found to have harassed. Most of these effects documented are results of the loss of financial resources as a result of the harassment. The loss of income, familial difficulties including separation or divorce, and a difficulty in procuring employment commensurate with experience and education are all additional effects of harassment experienced by the harasser.

Legal Effects

Conte (1997) and Burns (1995) provide thorough analyses of the legal issues surrounding sexual harassment. Conte states that a company assumes liability for the negligent hiring, retention, or supervision of someone known to sexually harass. Thus, if one is fired from an executive job for sexual harassment, future employers may be held liable for any future misconduct of this individual. This legal finding results in a hidden cost of sexual harassment: the cost of training this individual, plus the cost of finding a replacement, if that is possible (e.g., the owner of a small business). In many potential instances of alleged sexual harassment, the employer might avoid liability by developing strategies to prevent sexual harassment and to remedy it when it occurs. Thus, prevention and remediation are two areas in which employers can reduce their liability and expenses.

Organizational Costs

The economic costs of sexual harassment have been quantified in several reports. Excluding the cost of litigation, Wagner (1992) estimates that for Fortune 500 companies, the annual *per company* cost of sexual harassment as $6.7 million. Increases in sick days, medical claims, job turnover and retraining inflate the cost of sexual harassment. In the United States Merit System Protection Board (USMSPB, 1981) report, a job turnover rate of 10% was reported. This turnover results in the need for recruiting, hiring, and training new personnel, which adds to the cost (Gosselin, 1986). In the follow-up to the first Merit Systems Protection Board report, it was estimated that sexual harassment costs the federal government more than a quarter of a billion dollars over a two-year period (USMSPB, 1987).

WHAT CAN BE DONE WITH SEXUAL HARASSERS?

Conte (1995) presents several of the effects of sexual harassment, and hints at the outcome for the harasser. Typically, the harasser is provided the option of therapy, termination of the employment contract, or some other disciplinary measure. Although no treatment has been validated for the treatment of sexual harassers (O'Donohue, 1997) therapy can be a better option than firing the employee, leaving the maladaptive behavior in the harasser's repertoire, ready for the next victim, albeit in another setting. Moreover, there is no evidence that other disciplinary measures, such as leave without pay, are effective "treatments". Furthermore, there are examples of when firing the employee would not be a practical solution, e.g., the family owned small business. Were the owner of a mom-and-pop shoe store found liable for sexual harassment, the owner would most likely not choose to fire herself. Another example would be that of a uniquely qualified individual who is an irreplaceable asset to a corporation. If this person were found liable of sexual harassment, it is unlikely that he would be fired. On the other hand, companies left with the option of firing the harasser, are in a sense, passing the buck to the next unfortunate company; retaining the harasser and not providing any treatment; or providing the harasser with the option of a treatment which has not been shown efficacious for the reduction and/or hopeful elimination of their sexually harassing behaviors.

Laws and O'Donohue (1997) edited a book in which successful treatments for a variety of sexual misbehaviors, such as sexual assault, fetishism, exhibitionism and voyeurism were presented. The common theme throughout their book is that Relapse Prevention (RP) has been shown to be an efficacious approach to the treatment of a variety of sexual misbehaviors.

2

Relapse Prevention as an Appropriate Model for the Treatment of Sexual Harassers

RELAPSE PREVENTION AND HARM REDUCTION

There are several important similarities among sexual harassment and sexual offending which support the adaptation of the RP model to sexual harassers. First and foremost, they can be viewed as problems of self-control. Second, sexual harassers are more likely to sexually harass certain people in certain situations, thus an analysis of high-risk situations is appropriate. Third, research has indicated that cognitive distortions and the problem of immediate gratification (PIG) are issues in both sexual offending and sexual harassment. Fourth, both sexual harassment and sexual offending result in significant victimization of another individual, and thus victim empathy may be a point of intervention. Furthermore, there may be an element of fantasy to sexual harassment (Sandberg & Marlatt, 1989). Finally, another similarity for sexual harassment and sexual abuse is seen in the definitions of lapses and relapses. In both sexual harassment and abuse, a lapse can be defined as engaging in behavior related fantasy, willful elaboration, a formulation of a plan of action or engaging in the undesired behavior. A relapse would be the overt undesired behavior or a return to "baseline" or pre-treatment levels of function.

There are differences between sexual harassers and sexual abusers that dictate the need for some modifications of the RP model for work with sexual harassers. First, whereas the majority of sexual harassment cases adjudicated are done so in civil actions, the majority of sexual abuse cases are adjudicated in criminal courts (Conte, 1997). Thus, some of the contingencies in place in correctional settings will not exist in the treatment of sexual harassers. For example, there is a reduced likelihood of court ordered treatment, sentence reduction for completion of treatment, probation and parole supervision and an outpatient treatment program for sexual harassers. With sexual harassers treatment will be outpatient, whereas with sexual offenders treatment often takes place in prisons or civil commitment facilities.

Thus, it appears that treatments shown efficacious for sexual offending populations are promising foundations from which to build a manualized treatment for sexual harassers. Given the concerns expressed by Laws (1995) and the aforementioned differences between sexual offenders and sexual harassers, a modified adaptation of the RP model is appropriate for the treatment of sexual harassment.

The literature on the treatment of sexual offenders indicates several areas of concern when working with sexually offending populations. First among these is the motivation (Laws, 1989). An unmotivated client is unlikely to participate or succeed in this program. In addition a client denying their offense is also unlikely to participate successfully (Maletzky, 1997). O'Donohue and Letourneau (1993) describe a group treatment plan design to shift clients from denial to admitting their misbehavior. Thus, a program addressing sexual harassment, for which there may be strong denial would be strengthened by including this element, when appropriate. These issues are discussed in more depth later in this work.

PRE-TREATMENT INFORMATION

The client should be oriented to the psychoeducational nature of this treatment. It is an active, participatory process that requires quite a bit of effort. Informed consent must include this element.

Using the stepped-care method, a thorough review of available information (e.g., discovery) is necessary to determine the likely level of intervention. To determine the adequate dose, a review of the records may indicate the appropriate level of care. Although the following examples provide the most common examples of sexual harassment, they do not cover the full gamut; non-contact gender harassment, contact sexual harassment, *quid pro quo* sexual harassment, and sexual assault. For the client who is simply ignorant of the company policy and legal aspects of sexual harassment, and whose behavior was relatively minor, an informational video and directed readings may be an adequate level of intervention. For the *quid pro quo* harasser, particularly one who has multiple victims or incidents they will likely require the full dose offered through this text, and continued aftercare. For the person committing sexual assault at the workplace, in addition to any legal consequences, they would benefit from the full dose offered through this text, and formalized sex offender treatment, both individually and in groups.

3

Bicycles and Sexual Harassment

THE OFFENSE CHAIN, THE OFFENSE CYCLE, AND THE OFFENSE WHEEL

Before we describe the Offense Chain, Offense Cycle and Offense Wheel, we provide the definitions below for both you and your clients. Other authors have described the sequence of events that lead from a non-offending state to an offending state as a chain, cycle, or wheel. The cycle metaphor describes the chain below as a circular pattern of progressing from "normal" to misbehavior. A problematic element of this metaphor is the common application of the phrase "in cycle" to refer to the period of acting out. If the cycle metaphor is a accurate depiction, then the person would be "in cycle" all of the time, and in the offending aspect of the cycle when acting out. The cycle metaphor is most applicable when describing the maladaptive life cycle, in which sexualized coping is but one aspect of the "cycle." From the point of intervention, it may be useful to teach clients to intervene at any point on the chain, for breaking any link of the chain breaks the chain of re-offending.

- **Lapse**—An occurrence of an undesired behavior in the context of behavior cessation or reduction program (e.g., smoking a cigarette by the client in a smoking cessation program or visiting a bar by an alcoholic). A lapse is always less serious than a relapse.
- **Relapse**—A violation of the contract or terms of the behavior cessation or reduction program. Sometimes defined as a return to pretreatment levels of the problem behavior.
- **High Risk Situation**—A situation identified by client and therapist as one in which the client has a greater likelihood to experience a lapse or relapse. Part of a behavior chain that probabilistically

could lead to a lapse or relapse. Sometimes called danger zones, a risky situations, stop signs.

- **Setting the Stage**—Where high-risk situations typically refer to physical environments, there are private, internal experiences that may work like a high-risk situation. We refer to this aspect as setting the stage. For some, this may be unresolved anger, anxiety, and frustration. It will vary from client to client, however it is our experience that there oftentimes is an additive effect for the high-risk situation and setting the stage, in that either alone may not be sufficient for a relapse, but both in conjunction almost always leads to lapse and frequently to relapse.
- **Seemingly Irrelevant/Unimportant Decisions (SIDS/SUDS)**—Decisions early in a behavior chain that place the client in a high-risk situation, e.g., the pedophile deciding to buy milk from the market near the day care center rather than the market near the commercial district.
- **Problem of Immediate Gratification (PIG)**—The orientation to positive, usually smaller, short-term consequences with adverse, usually larger, long-term consequences, rather than to adverse or unwanted short-term consequences for a more beneficial long-term consequence. For example, eating the cake today instead of losing weight tomorrow.
- **Abstinence Violation Effect (AVE)**—The AVE occurs when a client lapses and irrationally concludes that the lapse is so severe, that they may as well relapse (e.g., since I broke the rule and I had one shot of whiskey, I may as well finish the bottle); a form of perfectionist or "all or none" thinking. Sometimes called the 'what the hell' phenomenon.
- **Offense Chain, Offense Cycle, Offense Wheel**—A pattern of behavior ranging from the non-offending (abstinent) through SIDs and setting the stage, High risk situation, PIG, lapse, relapse, AVE and return to abstinence. The sequence is variable both within and between harassers. For some, the PIG may occur between lapse and relapse, and for others it may occur before the lapse.

While in figure 3.1, Abstinence—Non-offending-"Faking Normal" appear as the endpoints, the person's experience may place them at different points along the chain during "baseline" and they will be in flux over time, such that an any observation over the course of the day or week may find them at a variety of points along the chain.

For each client, the offense chain will be different. And within each client's range of behavior, the chain will be different. It is crucial that you work with the client to identify all offenses of record, and off-the-record offenses, to prepare a fully informed offense cycle. Within the context of

Abstinence – Non-Offending – "Faking Normal"

→ SIDs

→ Setting the Stage

→ High Risk Situation

→ PIG

→ Lapse

→ Relapse

→ AVE

→ Abstinence – Non-Offending -"Faking Normal"

→ SIDs

→ Setting the Stage

→ High Risk Situation

→ PIG

→ Lapse

→ Relapse

→ AVE

→ Abstinence – Non-Offending-"Faking Normal"

Figure 3.1. Offense chain and maladaptive cycle

ethical requirements to report certain types of offending, you can work with the client to identify common themes, situations and elements to provide the full background from which to sketch the offense chain.

Example: Although brief, the following scenario provides some real-life examples of what we have seen in this area. While all clients will be different, this exercise should provide some useful examples of identifying these problems as they may occur. The examples used in this text are an amalgam based on experiences with clients. These have been modified so to not reveal any actual identifying information about the individual, their workplace, their victims, or their experiences.

Robert is a 33-year-old, college educated information technology specialist at a moderately sized company in a city on the west coast. He has worked for the company for 6 years, recently promoted from IT assistant to specialist, and having previously worked in a similar capacity for small companies across the southwestern United States. He is married, and his wife of 4 years is expecting their first child. Three separate complaints have been made to the HR department in the last 6 months related to

Robert's behavior. One the first occasion he is alleged to have repeatedly brushed his arm across the breasts of a coworker under the guise of solving a computer problem. The second report details Robert's placing a hand on a female coworker's thigh under the guise of lifting himself from a seated position on the floor under her desk. In the third complaint, he is reported to have again placed his hand on the thigh of a female coworkers while lifting himself from the floor, only to have his hand 'slip' to her crotch, and while trying to 'steady' himself, surreptitiously grab her breast with his other hand. Robert presents in your office after the company recommend that he seek professional intervention as part of a probationary period while the allegations are under investigation.

In the interview, you discover the following: Robert reveals that he and his wife have been having financial difficulties related to the pregnancy. As a result, Robert reports that he has been less attracted to his wife. Your review of the records indicates that all of the three complainants were temporary workers, young, and had auburn or brunette hair. Robert has told you that in his prior workings with each of three victims, he had engaged in banter that had contained occasional sexual innuendo.

For Robert's situation we'll define the terms as they relate to him:

- **Lapse**—engaging in banter that contains sexual innuendo
- **Relapse**—inappropriate physical contact with coworker
- **High Risk Situation**—being in close quarters with dark-haired, young, female, temporary workers
- **Setting the stage**—not feeling attracted to his spouse
- **SIDs**—Deciding to be seated on the floor to address the computer problem, deciding to stand in such a way as to necessitate a reach across his victim
- **PIG**—For Robert, it probably felt better to have the immediate gratification from touching the attractive young temp, then to address the problems he was having at home with his spouse
- **AVE**—having already touched the thigh of a coworker, Robert escalated into touching both her crotch and breast
- **Offense chain**—in looking at Robert's case, we can see that his problems at home set the stage for his offense. This is one area of intervention. Second, we see that Robert tends to be most at risk when in close quarters with attractive, dark-haired temps. Third, Robert's SIDs make his high-risk situations even more dangerous, as he sets himself up to make touching easy. He also pre-victimizes his coworkers by assessing their willingness to engage in sexual talk. We also notice an escalating pattern of behavior from the early report to the third report.

4

Comorbid Disorders

This section reviews the impact mental disorders may have on addressing the concerns of sexual harassment. We have found that in some cases, the harasser may deftly avoid addressing their sexual misbehavior by attending only to comorbid concerns. While it may be necessary to address these comorbid concerns, and sometimes a prerequisite, the therapist must eventually return to the problem of sexual harassment.

The first organizing principle in this area is for the therapist to assess the relationship between the harassing behaviors and the comorbid disorders. For example, is the depression the natural consequence of having hurt another, suffered humiliation and loss of status, or, does depression set the stage for the acting out that led to the charges of sexual harassment? We have seen other disorders fall into similar pathways. Anxiety can be the result of, or an enabling precursor of, sexual harassment.

This issue becomes a bit more thorny around two domains. The first is personality disorders, and the second is chemical dependence. Each presents unique challenges, and has been subject of NIMH-funded investigations. For the therapist, your challenge is to address the therapy-interfering behaviors that these issues present so that you can then effectively engage in the treatment provided in this manual. For example, the client displaying behaviors consistent with Borderline Personality Disorder can likely be expected to have sufficient distress within the therapeutic relationship to present challenges to the initial establishment of rapport. In such a case, Linehan's Dialectical Behavior Therapy (Linehan, 1993) may need to be employed before or in conjunction with this treatment before any strong gains can be anticipated with the sexual harasser.

What may be even more challenging than the client with Borderline symptomatology is the client who demonstrates psychopathy and/or antisocial personality disorder. Without an effective intervention demonstrated for psychopathy and anti-social personality disorder, the clinician is left to appeal to those features of the client's personality that may be drawn to the benefit of the intervention. In essence, if "punishment" based consequences are not impactful for the psychopathic or anti-social client, the clinician needs to orient the client towards the self-serving benefits of treatment. The therapist may also be faced with the need to reconceptualize the problem from one of eliminating the behavior and returning the client to the workplace to reducing the frequency and severity of the problem behavior (e.g., Harm Reduction), and managing the occurrences of these outbursts by reducing the likelihood of the problem through job placement and physical interventions.

Chemical dependency can often work as a combination of mood disorder and personality disorder. The substance abuse may work differently for different clients; it may be a predisposing, stage-setting disinhibitor, a form of liquid solace, or all of these. However, we recommend concomitant substance abuse treatment as self-control and all new learned skills are solvable in alcohol and other drugs.

Even though the client may claim that 'were it not for the (insert comorbid disorder here) they would not have sexually harassed, the therapist cannot rely on that as an accurate assessment. This form of denial and minimization is nothing but, and sometimes works on the novice therapist. The therapist would be remiss to only treat the comorbid concern and leave the sexual misbehavior unchecked. In this case, the therapist would be wise to address the denial and minimization, and present the need for the sexual harassment intervention as described in the denial and minimization section of this manual.

5

Treatment Modules

MODULE 1: ASSESSMENT

Notes: As this is the first module, there is neither opportunity for review of old material, nor will there be any integration of old and new material. Instead, this module serves to direct both your, and the client's attention toward the most important issues and procedures of Relapse Prevention (RP).

Inclusionary criteria for participation in therapy may be: self-reported willingness to participate in therapy and having been found to have sexually harassed. Exclusionary criteria for participation in therapy may be: acute comorbid mental disorder, e.g., parasuicidal behaviors, psychosis, etc. that will interfere with treatment.

Focus

The goal of any assessment procedure is to glean information that will speak to treatment issues. Thus, in the case of sexual harassers, there is a clear need for the therapist to have a broad understanding of the presenting problem, contexts in which it occurs, experienced outcomes, coping strategies, motivation for treatment and level of denial. To make the assessment more comprehensive, it is recommended that the nature and detail of the harasser's reports be compared with victim statements, sexual harassment investigation reports, and appropriate assessment devices. The therapist should also conduct a thorough psychological diagnostic assessment to rule in or to rule out other psychological problems, particularly those that could interfere with effective treatment.

The client will be oriented to the RP model; including a brief overview of the theoretical aspects of RP, and the mechanics of the program.

For example, the therapist will help the client define instances of lapses and relapses. The therapist should also orient the client to the active requirements of RP, such as homework.

Skills & Techniques

Motivation Ratings

Motivation Ratings, George & Marlatt (1984)

George and Marlatt found that participants' self-reports of their degree of motivation to change were a useful predictor of short and long-term therapy outcome. A client self-report of low motivation for participation in therapy would indicate that motivational interviewing is an appropriate intermediary step. Motivational interviewing is discussed briefly in Module 3. Please use attached Handout 2 to track motivation over time.

Denial and Minimization

Self-report Sexual Harassment Inventory (SRSHI), O'Donohue, Fitzgerald & Brunswig (1999)

The scale is based on Fitzgerald and colleagues' Sexual Experience Questionnaire (1988, 1998). It is to be used to attempt to delineate the client's range and extent of sexual harassment behaviors. It can also be used to assess changes in reported sexually harassing behaviors, i.e., decreases in minimization or shift from denial to admittance. To buttress the information reported in this scale, self-reports should be compared to workplace evaluations and victims' reports whenever possible. Reminders of when and how to obtain and use workplace performance reports are presented through the treatment modules. This scale will be a useful indicator of change pre- and post- for Overcoming Denial and Minimization. This scale is included as Handout 3.

Workplace Performance

Supervisor reports of lapses and relapses are to be used to compare the validity and accuracy of the self-report information gathered in the questionnaires. And as mentioned above, supervisor reports can also be used to assess any denial and minimization when used in conjunction with the self-report measures described here. To obtain this information you will need a release of information specific the information to be released, the intended use of the information, and if necessary consent to openly discuss the information with the supervisor. The information may be contained in the client's personnel file, or, depending on the nature of the organization, formal reports filed in different departments.

Sexual Harassment Knowledge Questionnaire

This measure assesses the client's knowledge of several issues pertaining to sexual harassment. Included in this measure are definitional measures, contextual questions, and questions relating to legal standards. This is included for frequent use with the client, and a score of 100% is necessary, but not sufficient, condition for termination. Correct answers may vary based upon jurisdiction. Please contact author (brunswig@unr.nevada.edu) for questions related to this questionnaire.

Sexual Harassment Myth Acceptance

Sexual Harassment Myth Acceptance, O'Donohue & Dubois (in preparation).

This scale measures the degree to which a person believes false information concerning sexual harassment. O'Donohue & Dubois are currently investigating the psychometric properties of this scale. This scale can be used in conjunction with the Hostility Towards Women scale for the evaluation of the effectiveness of Myth Acceptance, Cognitive Distortions and Negative Attitudes Towards Women. This scale is included as Handout 5.

Hostility Towards Women

Hostility Toward Women, Check & Malamuth (1983).

This scale measures the construct of anger towards women (Check & Malamuth, 1983). Malamuth (1986) reported an alpha coefficient for this scale of .89. This self-report measure can be completed by the client and scored by the clinician. This scale has shown to be predictive of inappropriate behaviors towards women and can be used as a pre-post indicator of change for Attitudes Towards Women.

Empathy

Victim empathy is a common element in sex offender treatment. It is argued that it is a lack of empathy towards that victim that is an enabling factor in the offending. That is, were the offenders aware of the impact their behavior had on the victim, they would be less likely to offend. As it relates to your client, empathy can be tracked using Handout 6.

Outcome Expectancies

Outcome Expectancies, Bandura 1977;
O'Donohue, Penix & Brunswig (under review).

Bandura (1977) suggested that ratings of perceived likelihood of outcomes on 10-point Likert scales could track outcome expectancies. We have used Outcome Expectancies ratings to assess the perceived likelihood of outcomes such as guilt, shame, worries about sexually transmitted diseases, pregnancy, likelihood of legal problems, career and reputation being negatively affected on 10-point Likert scales that range from "I would not at all expect that this would happen" to "I would completely expect that this would happen". This measure can be a useful assessment tool evaluating pre- and post-reports for Outcome Expectancies and the Problem of Immediate Gratification. More realistic expectations of positive and negative outcomes can be an indicator of important changes. Unchanging expectations can be an indicator of a continued need of focus on Outcome Expectancies.

General Assessment

It is important to understand who your client is and how he came to be where he is today. Thus, you should also conduct a general psychosocial assessment of your client's history, strengths and weaknesses, his goals, current living and mental health environments, problems at work, home, church, and community, and any other relevant issues. Use information obtained here to set the context and modify the application of relapse prevention treatment that follows.

Functional Assessment

Functional assessment involves reviewing the client's experience of sexual harassment for both intended and unintended outcomes, as well as obvious and subtle outcomes. The rationale behind functional assessment is that people do things because they work, or work in similar situations, or worked previously in the same or similar situations. Functional assessment then becomes an analysis of what "works" for the client. There are experimental methods for functional assessment (sometimes called functional analysis) in which the experimenter removes one possible consequence and evaluates the stability of the behavior (e.g., when we teach parents not to give in when the child tantrums, does the tantrum eventually cease?). In the workplace, we can rarely set up such a situation. Instead, we are left with Monday morning quarterbacking in that we rely on the client's report of intent and outcome to discern common themes and experiences. Our experience is that clients can be of assistance in this endeavor, in that they are often aware of the outcomes of their behavior, though often lacking insight into alternatives.

It is important for the client and clinician to be oriented towards this perspective. While a detailed historical analysis may yield long-standing patterns of misogyny, coupled with poor modeling, and enabling strained attachments, there is often something in the current environment that evokes and maintains the problem behavior. Some common motivations are escape and avoidance, attempts to engage others, attempts to enlist social support, attempts at expressing emotion, and sexual gratification. Here's an example:

Clarence was the kid in middle school who used to snap the bra straps on the girls sitting in front of him. He hadn't ever learned any other techniques for getting the girls to talk to him, and these attempts, while initially successful in gaining attention, did not work in the long-term to establish meaningful conversation and relationships. Instead, he found himself alienated from his female peers, and without much practice at successful conversation initiation. Fifteen years later, his skills set has not improved much, and his facility at engaging females in conversation is still awkward, often offensive, and in two cases, merited charges of sexual harassment. While in middle school he would snap the bras, his current charges stemmed from commenting on the bras worn by female peers and in one situation, asking a coworker if she was wearing a bra. In Clarence's case, functional analysis led us to the following:

- Clarence was attempting to start conversation
- While the attempts seemed sexual in nature; there was no arousal on his part
- Clarence was aware of the harmful impact his behavior had on others
- Clarence was often frustrated with himself for his awkwardness and harmful impact on female peers
- Clarence lacked effective social skills for his needs
- Clarence never learned alternatives, and the skills he did have often prevented him from having opportunities to practice other ways of engaging others.

Anthony is a middle-aged man who has never really felt comfortable around people in general, and met diagnostic criteria for schizotypal personality disorder. He is a wiz with actuarial tables, and is very successful in the insurance industry. Unfortunately for Anthony, he did something quite similar to Clarence. Rather than snap the bras of his female coworkers, he would simply comment on the visibility, color, lines, or possible absence of a bra on his female coworkers. This worked quite well for

Anthony, in that it quickly ended conversation initiated by females, which relieved the distress he experienced in social situations. In Anthony's case, his sexual harassment charges stemmed from such an interaction. While Anthony's behavior was quite adaptive given his wish to be left alone, it was maladaptive in its impact on others. In Anthony's case, functional analysis led us to the following:

- Anthony's wish to escape social interactions was the primary motivation for his sexual comments
- Anthony did not have any apparent sexual interest in his coworkers
- Anthony found that his comments were often immediately effective in the short term
- Anthony's discomfort around people prevented him from engaging previous therapy
- Anthony desired, but did not have alternatives that would allow him to escape a social situation without hurting others.

Our third example is Lucas. Around age 15, Lucas noticed that he was unusually attracted to female lingerie, specifically brassieres and lingerie in the brassiere family. He managed to function quite well in the work place, though at times he found himself aroused when a female coworker had aspects of her bra exposed. Lucas report that it could be anything from an exposed strap on the shoulder, to a hint of the cup should a coworker lean over, exposing a glimpse of fabric. He was charged with harassment for "leering" at a female coworker while telling her that her bra was "very, very pretty." In Lucas' case, functional analysis revealed the following:

- Lucas' attention towards brassieres was primarily sexual
- Lucas was generally able to manage his fetish at work
- Lucas did not have much practice at being aroused and not acting upon his arousal
- Lucas was somewhat aware of the impact he had on others, but was primarily motivated by the discomfort he experienced by being aroused and unable to manage that arousal.

In these cases, we have similar, and sometimes identical behaviors. However, the motivations behind them were quite different, and functional analysis led us to discover these differences. This analysis highlights one of the problems with cookie-cutter interventions, which we are hoping to avoid with this manual. The intent is that with a well-informed assessment, this manual can be tailored to each client's need. In the first two examples provided above, the clinician may want to first turn towards the social skills section, as both Clarence and Anthony needed social skills. However, while Clarence needed conversation initiation skills, Anthony needed conversation cessation skills. As we highlight in that section, initiation and cessation are two related, yet different skill sets. We also highlighted Lucas' problem in that while he had the social skills to start and stop conversations, he did not have the skills needed to manage his sexuality and arousal in the workplace. In his case, elements of Relapse Prevention and Harm Reduction would be more helpful than a social skills-based intervention.

In sum, we have three examples of the same behavior being motivated by three distinct factors: attempts to engage others, attempts to avoid others, and attempts at managing sexual arousal. While the topography of the behavior was identical from case to case, the function of each behavior was unique. Functional analysis informed this difference, and thereby informed the intervention.

It will be helpful to orient the client towards this form of analysis, as they may see other aspects in their lives where their needs are being unmet due to similar difficulties as those expressed related to their sexual harassment. The client may be struggling with issues such as peer rejection, intimacy, or sexual identity issues, to name only a few. By assessing the function of their misbehavior, the client may identify the need that they are attempting to meet with their misbehavior.

At the same time we explore the problem issues, we will begin to ask the client to do things differently. They will be swimming in uncharted waters, without their usual safety measures. When you ask a client to abandon their defenses, there is a sense of vulnerability that is often accompanied by flight, threats, fear, or a host of other forms of angstladen acting out. General psychoeducation related to coping skills may be of benefit early on as the client progress through this self-exploration and development. Growing pains are to be expected for both client and clinician, and it is important for both to have the requisite and helpful support through this process. Acceptance and Commitment Therapy (ACT; Hayes, Strosahl & Wilson, 1999) and Functional Analytic Psychotherapy (FAP; Kohlenberg & Tsai, 1991) may provide useful adjunctive therapy in these areas.

Treatment Planning

Treatment plans vary widely from institution to institution and therapist to therapist. In general, treatment plans involve identifying strengths and weaknesses, problems of deficits and excesses, interventions, goals, and timelines.

Treatment needs that should be in every plan include:

Problems:

1) Has sexually harassed

2) Lack of effective relapse prevention plan
3) Lack of skills for effectively negotiating daily living

Goals:

1) Eliminate claims of sexual harassment
2) Develop relapse prevention plan
3) Implement relapse prevention plan in daily living

Intervention:

1) Completing RP therapy for sexual harassers
2) Work collaborative with therapist to develop plan
3) Work with therapist, support group and human resource personnel to implement plan effectively
4) Effective treatment for other comorbid problems related to sexual harassment

The treatment plan will be individualized for every client based upon his or her needs and issues. However, since they have presented with a need for treatment for this specific behavior problem, these three issues should be included in each plan. Other issues such as chemical dependency, social skills deficits, marital discord, and paraphilias may also be of concern and related to these issues.

Schedule	
35%	Rapport Building Introduce self Appreciate client willingness to engage problem Discuss confidentiality Orient to assessment and treatment
65%	Introduce Assessment Explain procedure Explain treatment utility of each questionnaire Define and provide examples of sexual harassment Treatment planning Answer any questions

Homework

Client completes questionnaires. Client is to write down in detail the act(s) of harassment that lead to presenting for treatment. The client is also to write all previous acts that meet the legal standard of sexual harassment.

Therapy Transcript

We will use Robert as an amalgam of several of our clients who have sought treatment after having adverse work consequences due to their sexually inappropriate behavior at the workplace. We will follow Robert through each of the modules, using therapy transcripts and data to illustrate the intervention as delivered. In following with our earlier example, Robert is a 33-year-old, college educated information technology specialist at a moderately sized company in a city on the west coast. He has worked for the company for 6 years, recently promoted from IT assistant to specialist, and having previously worked in a similar capacity for small companies across the southwestern United States. He is married, and his wife of 4 years is expecting their first child.

Three separate complaints have been made to the HR department in the last 6 months related to Robert's behavior. One the first occasion he is alleged to have repeatedly brushed his arm across the breasts of a coworker under the guise of solving a computer problem. The second report details Robert's placing a hand on a female coworker's thigh under the guise of lifting himself from a seated position on the floor under her desk. In the third complaint, he is reported to have again placed his hand on the thigh of a female coworker while lifting himself from the floor, only to have his hand "slip" to her crotch, and while trying to "steady" himself, surreptitiously grab her breast with his other hand. Robert presented in our office after the company recommended that he seek professional intervention as part of a probationary period while the allegations are under investigation.

A general psychosocial interview revealed the following:

- Robert is the second of three boys born to an intact nuclear family. Robert's mother met diagnostic criteria for alcohol dependence prior to Robert's tenth birthday. Robert's parents divorced when he was 17 years old, and he received mental health counseling through his high school at that time. He was arrested once for possession of marijuana at age 20, and the charge was later dismissed. He does not meet diagnostic criteria for depression, any of the anxiety disorders, substance abuse or Axis II issues.
- Robert's general problem-solving strategy appears to be one of avoidance in which he reports to passively avoid problems until others solve them, or that they simply "pass on their own." Other than his current situation, he has generally received positive evaluations from previous employers.
- Robert reports that he and his wife have been having financial difficulties related to the pregnancy. As a result, Robert reports that he

has been less attracted to his wife. A review of the records indicates that all of the three complainants were temporary workers, young, and had auburn or brunette hair. Robert tells us that in his prior workings with each of three victims, he had engaged in banter that had contained occasional sexual innuendo. At the conclusion of the orientation interview, we closed with the following interchange:

T So in review, here's where we are; you've discussed the three allegations and said that you want to stay out of trouble. What I need to do now is get more information about what's going on for you, so I can provide the most efficient help. It's like when you go to the doctor and she asks for a blood test to help find out how you're doing, I have some questionnaires that will help me see how you're doing.

R Ok. How long will they take?

T It will probably take a couple of hours, and it's best if you fill them in a quiet area, without many distractions. Some ask general information questions, some are specific to sexual harassment, but all of them will help me out. If possible, please complete them in my office after we're done talking here, and then leave them with my receptionist.

R Why's that? I don't know if I can get them done that fast.

T I'd like a chance to review them before our next session, so we can go over your answers, and any questions you have, at that time.

R Ok, I'll try.

T There is one other thing.

R There's always another thing.

T Chuckle, well... you're right. Part of the treatment for this problem, for sexual harassment, involves a good deal of homework. It's not just the hour a week that you come in here—you need to be working on this stuff out there. Just practicing the good stuff in the therapy room doesn't tell me that you can do the good stuff at work. So, I am going to ask you to do a lot of things, sometimes homework, sometimes exercises.

R Huh?

T I'm doing a lot of the talking here, and that's pretty common in the first couple sessions, let me rephrase that last one. You're going to have to do homework as part of therapy, and some of the homework might be written and some of it will be activities—doing things, going places, watching tapes; things like that.

R Ok, that makes sense.

T All right, so I've got a packet of questionnaires for you, and there's this other thing.

R Right, the other thing.

T The other thing is what I'll call a disclosure.

R Like the earning statements the finance boys do at work.

T Something like that. What are the earning statements like?

R It's where we make a report for the shareholders about the money—what's coming in, what's going out, are we meeting projections, things like that.

T Well, this disclosure is going to be a little like that. Like the shareholders need to know where the money is, I need to know what happened. That's the important part of my job. It's sort of like, you're walking along and suddenly you've fallen into a hole—my job is twofold, first, help you get out of the hole, and two, figure how to help you avoid holes for next time. For me to do that, I need to know ...

R You need to know how I got into the hole.

T Exactly.

R Those damn temps took it the wrong way.

T Whoa-whoa—let's hold off on that for now. The homework exercise is for you to tell me your side of things. I want to hear what you think happened—for each of the three events that we've talked about. And then I'd like you to include any others that aren't part of those three.

R What? You want what?

T I want you to do a couple things—first, tell me about the three events with the temps that we've already talked about. What happened, where you were, what you did, things like that. Then I want you to include any other incidents that haven't been reported.

R I'm not doing that. I'll get busted. This sucks. You want me to incriminate myself. Are you going to report this? What the hell?

T Ok, let me backtrack a quick second. I need to know about other events, but you can be honest and vague at the same time. For example, you can give the specifics of the event, without telling where you worked, if it was reported, the other person's name, the exact location. That way I know what you did—I know what the harassment looked like, but I don't have to break confidentiality, because your company, yourself and I agreed that I'd only report new acts of harassment if you told me of a specific event on a specific date with a specific victim. Remember the goal is here for you to have a great future life, because this sort of thing never happens again. I don't want to play cop—it's not my job.

R But this is acting like a cop.

T Yeah, I can see that. So, we figure out a way for me to get the info I need, and for you to protect yourself.

R I don't want to be in any more trouble.

T I don't want you in any more trouble either.

R Good. Ok, so I just need to write down my side of things about the three things with the temps, the things that got me busted.

T Yeah.

R And then you want me to write about other times—even if they were reported, or not reported, or anything—all of 'em.

T Yes, all of 'em.

R And you won't report them.

T If you don't give me the specifics, I don't have anything to report.

R All right.

T Ok. And you know what—you don't have to do this right the first time.

R Hunh, so I'm going to have to do this again.

T Yes, you're going to have to work.

R All right, let's get on with it.

MODULE 2: UNDERSTANDING SEXUAL HARASSMENT

Focus

The focus of this module to inform the therapist as to how to correct any knowledge deficits in the harasser that may have led to the sexual harassment. By this time, the client should have had an opportunity to review the company policy, but may not know the law, and the applications of both policy and law as it relates to their experience. This module includes a large portion of psychoeducation and didactic instruction. It is important for the therapist to have reviewed the client's company policy, as well as the earlier chapters of this work before this module. Consistent with the stepped-care approach, this module may be the necessary and sufficient dose for the relatively minor cases or for those simply ignorant of the policy, law and consequences. Throughout this section and following, the client should be reminded that ignorance of the policy and law does not free them from responsibility.

Skills & Techniques

Review the client's scores on the Sexual Harassment Knowledge Questionnaire. Correct and explain any errors. In review incorrect responses, look for any cognitive biases, thinking errors, logical problems, and knowledge deficits that may have influenced the selection of the incorrect answer.

Provide the client with a copy of The FAQs of Sexual Harassment. Using the information provided in this handout, as well as the earlier chapters of this work, provide definitions and ask the client to demonstrate comprehension by providing examples of:

- *Quid pro quo*
- Gender harassment
- 3rd party harassment
- Hostile environment
- Reasonable person standard
- Company policy
- Effects and consequences
    - For the victim
    - For the harasser
- Legal effects
    - Criminal
    - Civil
- Organizational effects
- Cost to company

Useful Metaphors

My Car Broke Down!

In this metaphor, describe an experience in which you, or the client had their car break down. Describe to the client alternate ways to get to and from work, or whatever the appointed rounds may have been that day. Typically the client will agree that the obligations of the day were to be met, and that the lack of transportation was not a legitimate excuse to shirk responsibility. The comparison is then made between knowledge of sexual harassment law and the car. Even though the client was lacking both, the client is still responsible for completing the work tasks.

Murder and Manslaughter

This metaphor may be too extreme for some clients, and its use is left to discretion of the clinician. In most jurisdictions, the difference between charges of murder and manslaughter center on premeditation or intent. This metaphor maybe used for clients who claim that their experience was one of intent; that their victims misperceived intent. In legal cases, the intent may mitigate the type and length of sentence, but murder and manslaughter both decree culpability. Even if the driver did not mean to kill the pedestrians in an accident, the driver may still be responsible. A similar example can be found with firearms in foreign countries. While handguns may be readily available in the United States, their unfettered possession in Canada and Mexico result in criminal prosecution. Ignorance of this law rarely frees the American from responsibility. These metaphors are also useful in the next module, Overcoming Denial and Minimization.

The Flashlight

In this metaphor, sexual harassment knowledge is likened to a flashlight that can be of use for the client to successfully navigate a difficult environment: the workplace. Start by comparing the workplace to an obstacle course. There are hoops through which one must jump, hurdles to clear, duties to avoid and some duties to assume. Now ask the client to see that same obstacle course in the dark. The likelihood of avoiding stumbles increases dramatically when walking through a darkened area beset with obstacles. In this case, the knowledge provides a source of light with which the client can better navigate this obstacle course.

The Wrong X-Ray

In this metaphor, describe a doctor about to perform an amputation on a diseased foot. The doctor would need to know which foot is to be amputated before she can do the correct surgery. If she's given the wrong x-ray, she can perform the techniques of the surgery flawlessly, and still get into trouble. Likewise for our clients, their decisions may be perfectly logical, but if they base their decisions on the wrong information, their follow-through on the information may get them into trouble.

Schedule

20%	Review Answer any questions left over from assessment. Review completion of all assessment information. Discuss information from assessment related to Sexual Harassment Knowledge Questionnaire.
25%	Review Sexual Harassment Knowledge Questionnaire Correct and explain any errors.
15%	Review The FAQs of Sexual Harassment
30%	Quiz client of comprehension of FAQs
10%	Overview homework

Metaphors from the Myth Acceptance and Cognitive Distortions Module may also be of assistance in this area.

Homework

The client should write an essay detailing their experience, highlighting any knowledge deficits that led to their experience(s) of sexual harassment. They can also be directed to write a paper on current legal standards and issues, which could require the use of EEOC information, library and Internet research.

Repeat or Proceed Decision Tree

- If the client cannot provide definitions and examples of, *quid pro quo*, gender harassment, third party harassment, hostile environment, reasonable person standard, company policy, effects and consequences for the organization, victim and harasser, and describe the possible criminal and civil repercussions, the client is to repeat this module.

Therapy Transcript

T Good to have you back, any new problems over the past week?

R Not really. I've been minding my ps and qs at work, and things have been going well at home.

T Ok, what I want to do today is review one of the questionnaires you filled out before, and I wanted to give you a handout to help in this area.

R Ok—which one?

T The Sexual Harassment Knowledge Questionnaire.

R That was tough—some of those I didn't know and I just guessed.

T To be honest with you, I didn't know this stuff as well as I should have before I started learning about sexual harassment. The legal standards have changed, and they can vary from place to place.

R Well, and some of the stuff, I mean, I don't want to shirk responsibility on this, but my sexual harassment training at work was something like, 'it's bad, don't do it.'

T Unfortunately, that happens quite a bit. Anyway, we're swaying a tad bit. One thing stood out in the questionnaire.

R What's that?

Robert's Sexual Harassment Knowledge Questionnaire	True or False
1. Sexual harassment is defined as any unwanted sexual attention.	T
2. As long as you didn't mean to sexually harass a co-worker your behavior is not considered sexual harassment.	T
3. Sexual harassment is not a violation of a person's civil rights.	F
4. The law considers the intent of the person committing the sexually harassing action in determining if sexual harassment has occurred.	T
5. As long as you don't touch a woman, you can say things like "women don't make good managers," and not be committing any type of sexual harassment.	F
6. Sexual harassment is a violation of both civil and criminal law.	T
7. Telling dirty jokes at work is okay, and not considered sexual harassment.	F
8. Asking a woman to have sex with you in exchange for a raise or promotion is considered *quid pro quo* sexual harassment.	T
9. Rating a woman on a scale from 1 to 10 in front of other women would not be considered sexual harassment under the current laws.	T
10. Although sexual harassment is illegal, statements like, "If an equally qualified man and woman apply for a job, the man should get the job," are okay.	T
11. Statements like "men are stupid" are a form of sexual harassment called gender harassment.	F
12. Even if you sexually harass someone you can't be fired or demoted.	F
13. As long as you can prove a person was "asking for it" your actions cannot be considered sexual harassment.	T
14. If you can prove that your attention was wanted then your actions will not be considered sexual harassment in a court of law.	T
15. Gender harassment, for example, saying "women don't belong in the workplace" is not legally considered sexual harassment.	F
16. Repeatedly asking someone out for a date who has said no, could be considered sexual harassment.	T
17. Even though the law states that any unwanted sexual attention is illegal, there are some forms of unwanted sexual attention that are not considered sexual harassment.	F

18. The reasonable woman standard, which means that any behavior a reasonable woman would see as sexual harassment is sexual harassment, has been upheld in court. F_____

19. As long as you don't see your actions as unwelcome then you are not engaging in sexually harassing behaviors. F_____

20. Rubbing a woman's shoulders is not sexual harassment as long as you are just trying to keep work a friendly place. T_____

21. Posting sexually explicit material in your office, such as "beefcake" posters is just harmless "girls' stuff" and not sexual harassment. F_____

22. A man can be sexually harassed by a woman or another man. T_____

23. As long as an offensive joke is sent via email, and not face-to-face, it is not sexual harassment. F_____

24. Third party harassment, in which someone denied a promotion due to a *quid pro quo* arrangement between two others, has been considered sexual harassment in a court of law. F_____

25. Even though he does not work for your company, the deliveryman can legally make claims of sexual harassment if he receives unwanted sexual attention while delivering a package to your workplace. T_____

26. If you are found responsible for an act of sexual harassment, the company for whom you work bears sole financial responsibility for any lawsuit. F_____

27. A woman cannot sexually harass another woman. F_____

28. Spreading a little sexual gossip about a co-worker can be considered sexual harassment. T_____

29. If your boss tells a risqué joke, you cannot be found to have sexually harassed if you tell the same joke to other coworkers. F_____

30. Giving a coworker a supportive swat on the bottom is an appropriate form of encouragement. F_____

T On two of the questions, 2 and 4 actually, you indicated that your intent would be an important factor in determining if what happened was sexual harassment.

R And, what, am I wrong?

T You are wrong, and that's the blunt truth.

R All right. If you say so.

T Nope. That's not going to cut it. What's the reason why? I'm concerned a little because you missed number 18, which would have helped.

R Well, I thought it was that if I was just trying to be nice, and she took it the wrong way, that I'd be safe.

T That's not how the law sees it, nor, I will add, does your company.

R I don't know. I'm stumped.

T Ok, if there are two people in the interaction, and our intent doesn't mitigate—it doesn't determine if it's harassment, what's left?

R Well, her reaction.

T Or more generally...

R Her.

T Yah. Let's explore that—

R Ok, I'm tying this into the first question, which I remember, and the policy from work—which is something like unwanted and unwelcome are the two key things.

T You're headed in the right direction, though the legal standard is a little more abstract.

R What would generally be unwanted to unwelcome?

T You're in the right ballpark. The standard, and again, this varies a bit from place to place, but the standard is what would a reasonable person, or a reasonable woman find? Would she find it offensive, unwanted, or unwelcome?

R How can I know what?

T Know what?

R What a reasonable woman would think? Isn't that part of my problem, that I can't figure out what's reasonable and what's not?

T That's part of why we're working on this.

R Grrr... I'm getting frustrated with this—it's like I'm in trouble for doing something I thought was maybe a little wrong, but I didn't think it'd be such a big thing, and I don't want to cause any more hurt, but I don't know the rules. It's like I'm in trouble for breaking a rule I didn't know existed, and I can't learn the rule.

T I'm getting that you're frustrated, and it makes sense, given your experience. However, that doesn't change that one, you didn't know the rules, and two, we're doing something about it.

R What do you mean?

T What we're doing is that learning process. Step one was to see what you know and what you did, step two is seeing what you usually do and how you work. After that, we work *together* to fill in any gaps in what you know and what you do.

R I'm following you on the first part—you're just saying the first part is correcting any ignorance on my part. What's the other?

T What you do based on that ignorance. It's like if a doctor had to perform a surgery to amputate a diseased limb. What would happen if the radiology department indicated that the disease, which you couldn't tell from the naked eye, was in the left foot, when in reality, it was in the right foot?

R Well, the doctor would probably cut off the wrong foot.

T True enough, but would the doctor make any mistakes in the surgery itself?

R Probably not, their only problem would be cutting off the wrong limb, I wouldn't expect them to make mistakes, if it was just based on bad info.

T And that may be what happened to you—

R You mean I got some bad info?

T You tell me, you're the one who wrote that your intentions are the important thing to consider in sexual harassment.

R Ah... slippery one there doc. I'm following you. So what else did I miss?

MODULE 3: OVERCOMING DENIAL AND MINIMIZATION

Focus

The next step is the evaluation and treatment of denial and minimization. This is to be done through the comparison of client report in the Self-Report Sexual Harassment Inventory and data gleaned through the supervisor reports and any sexual harassment investigation reports. Denial is seen when the client refuses to admit the occurrence of problem behavior of contrary evidence. An example of client denial would be a statement such as, "I never said what they say I did, Heck, I wasn't even in the room." Minimization can be seen in attempts to make the nature or consequences of the problem behavior seem less severe that they actually are. For example, a client may say, "she laughed at the jokes, so she must not have been as traumatized as her and her lawyer made her out to be." The focus of this section should be to help the client get to place in which they acknowledge the significance of both their actions and the consequences of those actions.

Skills & Techniques

Clients will be presented with any archival data that contradict their self-report. The focus of the O'Donohue and Letourneau's (1993) intervention was to overcome denial, help the client admit to the offense and be motivated to participate in therapy.

An adaptation of their techniques to the treatment of sexual harassment would include: presenting the probable outcomes of receiving versus not receiving treatment, e.g., gainful employment versus lower wage or no employment and likelihood and consequences of future instances of sexual harassment, e.g., if treated, lower likelihood of re-offense, if untreated, higher likelihood of re-offense and more severe consequences.

If the harasser is denying the offense, the second module will address these areas. In this module the therapist will use the intervention of motivational interviewing (MI). The clinician, if skilled in MI, can begin utilizing MI from the outset, although if the client is already motivated for therapy, MI might not be of any incremental utility. However, if after one session the client is still denying, it would be appropriate to utilize MI in a second Overcoming Denial and Minimization session, as MI has been shown effective in a variety other RP treatment evaluations (c.f., Bell & Rollnick, 1996; Heather, Rollnick, Bell & Richmond, 1996; Miller, 1996). This module will continue until the harasser admits to the harassment in a way that does not minimize the harassment or interfere with subsequent therapy. If the client does not admit to the harassment, or does not acknowledge both severity of their actions and their consequences, it is recommended that the client be returned to pre-treatment until such time as they are willing to admit to the nature and consequences of their actions. In doing such, the therapist may help the client come into contact with the natural contingencies for their behavior, such as an inability to find employment commensurate with their experience.

Useful Metaphors

The Impaired Detective

In this metaphor, the clinician is likened to a detective that is unable to gain access to the evidence. Consider a detective that cannot have crime scene reports, cannot have the medical examiner's report, fingerprint evidence, or take witness statements. That detective is not going to be able to "put it all together" to figure out what happened.

The Cook

In this metaphor, the clinician is compared to a cook that is allowed on three or four ingredients with which to prepare meals. Ask the client what they would expect if the chef had only salt, pepper, garlic, rice and chicken. Would the client eat at that restaurant? Would the client have a business meeting there? The more ingredients at the chef's disposal, the chef will be more enabled to fulfill the diners' needs.

The Pitcher

In this metaphor, the client is likened to the baseball catcher, and the clinician is the pitcher. The pitcher is limited by the calls the catcher is prepared

Schedule	
20%	Review Discuss information from Understanding Sexual Harassment Knowledge and Assessment Modules, (e.g., clarify the nature and purpose of assessment, clarify link from assessment to treatment, how sexual harassment myths will be addressed later) Answer any questions about Understanding Sexual Harassment and Assessment Modules
20%	Introduce Denial and Minimization Explain terms Explain importance of terms Show empathy to client related to difficulty of disclosure Answer any questions
40%	Denial and Minimization Compare client report with supervisor report and investigation report Ask client to resolve any discrepancies Praise client for honest report if applicable If discrepancies persist, provide client with additional SRSHI to be completed before next session. If discrepancies persist after the second SRSHI administration, the next session is to be conducted using the Motivational Interviewing techniques described above
20%	Review Review the session Outline homework to be completed (e.g., SRSHI) if necessary Describe next session

to make. If the catcher only calls for fastballs, the hitters will soon learn what to expect, and will soon be hitting everything thrown their way. Successful pitchers have a variety of pitches, and must work with the catcher to use the right pitch at the right time. If the catcher limits the pitches in the pitchers repertoire, the pitcher is limited in their ability to be effective.

The Football Team

In this example, the therapy process is likened to a football game. In this case, the client is the coach calling the plays. Each new disclosure is a new play. If the coach has only one or two plays, the team is going to lose. The more information the coach has at their disposal the better the team will do.

Homework

- Complete Self-report Sexual Harassment Inventory
- Continue written disclosure of harassment history

Repeat or Proceed Decision Tree

1) If client has discrepancies between supervisor report, SRSHI, and homework from Assessment Module, client is to repeat SRSHI and homework from Assessment module. For example, if the client's verbal, written and self-report data do not concur with documented investigation report, these discrepancies should be discussed with the client and the session repeated.
2) If client is still denying either the occurrence or severity of the offense(s) Module 2 is to be repeated using Motivational Interviewing. The client is to again complete the SRSHI and homework from the Assessment module.
3) If after a session of Motivational Interviewing, the client is still denying the occurrence or severity of the offense, therapy should be postponed until such time as the client admits to the occurrence and severity of the offense described in supervisor reports and investigational reports. However, if the client has moved from completely denying the occurrence of the event to minimizing the severity, (e.g., "I didn't do what they say happened" to "I know I shouldn't have said what I did, and I may have even touched here in a way she didn't want to be touched—that doesn't mean I should have to

go through all of this") the clinician may choose to proceed to Module 4. If the clinician proceeds to Module 4 without a full admission by the client, the clinician should endeavor to inform the client that admitting 3 of 30 acts of harassment is enough to begin treatment, that it does not qualify as a full acknowledgement of the occurrence and severity of their actions and that this is expected before treatment is completed.

Therapy Transcript

T Ok, so let's have a look at the disclosure assignment.

R The one where I was supposed to confess my sins.

T Or to put it another way, a chance for me to see what's going on for you.

R Yah yah. All right, here it is.

T Care to read it aloud?

R Not really.

T Try it.

R Ok. Number one. Really, I have to read this?

T I've found it works best that way.

R All right. Number one. Touching—I can't really remember the number of times I've rubbed up on, or grabbed accidentally a girl at school or on the bus or a concert or whatever. I mean, all the guys I knew in middle school and high school did it. I was horny all the time, and I just wanted a chance for some release. All right, there was this one time at camp when we were making posters for our concert. I was helping to put up this poster, and there was girl, she was shorter than me, she was trying to hold the poster up and use the staple gun to punch it in place. So I was coming up from behind her, and I grabbed a hold of the poster and told her to staple it in place. Well, I was, uhm, aroused, a little, and ya know, she had this tight little butt, and I just sorta of leaned in closer and told her that I was trying to keep my balance. I think she knew what was going on, coz she got a little red. I hadn't thought about that in a while, but mmm. Wow. Anyway, Number 2. I don't know how many times I did the 'over the keyboard move' in college. I t.a.ed intro to computer science a few times, and there are always some girls who didn't know what to do, so I'd always end up on the opposite side of their mouse or keyboard and have to reach

Robert's Self-Report Sexual Harassment Inventory

Using this scale, please indicate how often you have done the following

0 = never
1 = once or twice
2 = more than twice
3 = often
4 = many times

1. Have you ever been in a work situation where you habitually told your coworkers or supervisees sexually suggestive stories or offensive jokes? 1

2. Have you ever been a situation where you made crude and offensive sexual remarks either publicly (for example in the office), or to your coworkers or supervisees? 2

3. Have you ever been a situation where you treated your coworkers or supervisees "differently" because of their gender (i.e. mistreated, slighted, or ignored them)? 2

4. Have you ever been a situation where you were condescending toward your coworkers or supervisees or "put them down" because of their gender? 1

5. Have you ever been in a situation where you displayed, used, or distributed sexist or sexually suggestive materials (e.g. pictures, stories, or pornography)? 0

6. Have you ever been a situation where you made sexist remarks (e.g. suggest that women are too emotional to be scientists or to assume leadership roles)? 0

7. Have you ever been in a situation where you made unwanted attempts to draw coworkers or supervisees into a discussion of personal or sexual matters (e.g. attempted to discuss or comment on your sex life)? 2

8. Have you ever been a situation where you gave coworkers or supervisees unwanted sexual attention? 3

9. Have you ever been a situation where you attempted to establish a romantic sexual relationship with a co-worker or supervisee despite their efforts to discourage you? 0

10. Have you ever been a situation where you have continued to ask a co-worker or supervisee for dates drinks, dinner, etc., even though they had said "no"? 0

11. Have you ever been a situation where you touched a coworker or supervisee (e.g. laid a hand on their bare arm, put an arm around their shoulders) in a way that made them feel uncomfortable? 3

12. Have you ever been a situation where you made unwanted attempts to stroke or fondle a coworker or supervisee (e.g. stroking their leg or neck, touching their breast, etc.)? 3

13. Have you ever been in a situation where you made unwanted attempts to have sex with a coworker or supervisee that resulted in their pleading or physically struggling? 0

14. Have you ever been a situation where you made a coworker or supervisee feel like they were being subtly bribed for some sort of reward or special treatment to engage in sexual behavior? 0

15. Have you ever been in a situation where you made a coworker or supervisee feel subtly threatened with some sort of retaliation for not being sexually cooperative (e.g. the mention of an upcoming evaluation, review, etc.)? 0______

16. Have you ever been in a situation where you implied faster promotions or better treatment if a co-worker or supervisee was sexually cooperative? 0______

17. Have you ever been in a situation where you made it necessary for a coworker or supervisee to respond positively to sexual or social invitations in order to be well treated on the job? 0______

18. Have you ever been in a situation where you made a coworker or supervisee feel they would be treated poorly if they didn't cooperate sexually? 0______

19. Have you ever been a situation where you treated a coworker or supervisee badly for refusing to have sex? 0______

20. Have you ever sexually harassed a coworker, customer, or other woman in your workplace? 3______

21. Has anyone ever said you sexually harassed anyone in your workplace? 2______

across them to do whatever it is that they needed. There wasn't any really harm, they were just brushes or glancing touches. They probably didn't even know I was doing it. Anyway, I never really grabbed anyone until I started here. It just seemed like I needed an extra pop. Ok, so there are three here at work—work number 1: Michelle—same thing as I did in college. She was having some trouble manipulating a spreadsheet, in part due to some lame attempt she made to reconfigure her hardware set-up, anyway—that doesn't matter, she uhm, she was looking nice, she was wearing this shirt, top, whatever you call it, and it was very flattering on her. Oh wait, some background. One time, right after she first got here, she was in the break room talking with someone about her weekend. She had said to her friend that she had a disappointing date with the guy her friend had set up for her, and I said something like, "I can't imagine it being a bad date, as long as you were there." And her friend giggled, and she sorta blushed a little, I don't know. I didn't have a whole lot to do with her before the "incident." Anyway, on the day of the "incident" she was sitting there, looking all cute, and she smelled nice too. She had taken off her jacket, and was just looking good. I thought I'd have a chance to, you know, see how she felt, and I did. She was struggling with what I was saying, so I said, "let me show you" and I was on her left, and I reached over with my right hand and in doing so, the back of my right hand grazed both of her breasts and she sorta blushed and scooted her chair back, and I grabbed the mouse and sorta kept my arm below her keyboard. And I asked her to lean closer so she could see what I was doing, and that made her sorta uhm, press herself against me. And then she said, could I do it from the other side, and I said, "I never had a girl ask me that before" and she looked really embarrassed, and she said "no, I mean, what I meant was come over here so you don't have to reach." And I said ok, and went over the other side; and showed her how to do it.

T Ok. Let me stop you here, and let's go through this one.

R All right. I've got the other two to talk about.

T I know. So your report is that you grazed her breasts once, and then situated it so she had to press her breasts into your arm, and then you made an innuendo. You had previously made an innuendo to her before, and hadn't heard that she didn't like it, or that she had found it offensive.

R Yah, that's about it.

T All right. One of the things I said I'd do is compare your version with her version. The report I have says that she recalls 4 times that you had made comment that made her feel uncomfortable.

R Four? That's crap.

T All right, let me review. She reports the same one you did, with the "I can't imagine a bad date."

R Good, so I'm not trying to hide anything. What are the other three?

T Ok, she says there was one time when you were both riding the elevator up from the parking garage, and that you "invaded [her] personal space." It looks like this happened in late July.

R July ... oh, that. Gotcha ok.

T What?

R All right, ok, there was a day, it was a casual Friday, and she was wearing this loose fitting shirt thing, and I'm a tall guy, and I sorta scooted behind her and managed it so I could look down her shirt. I think that might be it. I mean the elevator wasn't very crowded, and I was being, you know, cool.

T So there was one. Any others you can recall?

R Uhm.

T Anything?

R Yah ... I uhm, how do I say this, I kneed her in the butt.

T You what?

R Yah, we were walking up stairs, and I was behind her, and she sorta paused on a step and I kept going and I ended up hitting her in the butt with my knee. I think I tried to steady her by putting my hand on her back. But seriously, I didn't mean that. I mean, come on, my knee?

T She reported that one. And that's about all she said on that. So it seems that's an accurate disclosure. It seems she also said, "what the hell was that for?" and that she told you to "knock it off."

R Well, that one was really an accident. It was nice, but an accident.

T Ok, calling it nice—that needs to stop.

R Oh. Well, uhm, what's the other one.

T She reports a time about a week before the one major incident in which you put your hand on top of her hand when she was using the mouse on her computer.

R Gotcha. Yup. I wasn't trying anything funny there. But I can see where she's coming from. I mean she's thinking I'm some sorta perv at this point. Ok, seriously, I'm not trying to leave anything out. I just wasn't thinking about all those. They didn't seem that big.

T And are they?

R I suppose so. I mean they don't seem like much to me, but yah, I did them.

T Ok, I'm going to have to throw a flag on this one. Hold on a second.

R All right.

T There are two issues I need to address when we do this. First—if there's any denial. Sometimes I have people in here that say, "No, I never did it." And you're not doing that.

R No, I know I screwed some things up; I'm trying to make it right.

T And that's a good thing—ok, so you're not denying what she's said. But you are minimizing a little bit.

R Miniwhattting?

T Minimizing—make it seem like a smaller thing that it is.

R I'm not following you.

T Ok, you know the saying, making a mountain out of a molehill?

R Yah.

T Minimizing is the opposite, making a molehill out of a mountain.

R Right. Ok, so I'm saying it's not as bad as it really is.

T Just so.

R So what do we do about it?

T I call it when I see it. I'm paying attention to the fact that you almost got fired, you embarrassed your wife and you really hurt these women.

R All right, so when I was just doing it.

T I think your words were, "they didn't seem like much to me."

R They don't.

T And is that accurate?

R Well, I guess it's a big deal. I mean, I'm shelling out the big bucks to see you aren't I?

T And again, here it is. You minimize the problem any time you discount the severity of the behavior, both in terms of how it impacts her, and how it is in it's own right.

R Ok... so if I make a joke, or make it seem like no big deal, I'm minimizing.

T Minimizing.

R Ok. Were there more?

T Yah, and there will continue to be more. Part of what we're going to do is come at this problem from a variety of ways. I can confront you when I see it, and we'll come at it some other ways too.

R Sounds like a plan. What about the questionnaires I did?

T It looks like you've been pretty consistent in what you've acknowledged in your disclosure and what you've reported here. Your most common harassments have been, let's see... "gave coworkers or supervisees unwanted sexual attention," "touched a coworker or supervisee in a way that made them feel comfortable," "you made unwanted attempts to stroke or fondle a coworker or supervisee," and, this was great to report this, 'have you ever sexually harassed a coworker."

R Well, I do want to do better. I said so on the motivation rating form. I want to stop doing this, I need help.

T And you're on your way towards getting that. There was something on the questionnaire that troubled me a little.

R What's that?

T Well, on #20, you endorsed 3, or "often" for how often you've sexually harassed, and on #21, you endorsed 2, or 'more than twice" for how may times you've been reported.

R That's because I've done way more than I've been busted for.

T That's what I thought, and that you're saying it is encouraging that you want to get better. So there's more.

R So, there's more ... the second victim, her name is Cassie.

T Well said, she is a victim, and she is a person.

MODULE 4: SKILLS TRAINING

Focus

The fourth module will involve social skills training. Harassers may be misperceiving both verbal and non-verbal behaviors by those in the workplace (McDonel & McFall, 1991; Penix and O'Donohue, in press). By training clients to accurately perceive verbal and non-verbal cues, the client should be better prepared to interact in the workplace environment without engaging in harassing behaviors. The client will also be taught pro-social skills that may serve as protective factors against future complaints of sexual harassment.

Skills & Techniques

An ideographic assessment should be used to learn which, if any, key social skill deficits are present. Deficits in perception, interpretation, response generation, enactment and evaluation will be discussed below (McDonel & McFall, 1991). Asking the client about situations in which they have had difficulty interacting with others, or situations in which they are uncomfortable can assess these deficits. These can also be assessed by role playing key situations and making inferences from the offense chain. Social skills training can be used to address these deficit areas. Clients and therapists will discuss the abstract principles of the particular class of social skills. The therapist will then model the specific set of social skills and the client will practice enacting these. The client and therapist will then role-play a situation that emphasizes the specific social skills relevant for the client. For example, the client and therapist may role-play joke-telling situations, socializing, or other critical situations common at the workplace. The therapist will then provide feedback for the client regarding the skills present and absent during the role-play. Repeated practice with performance feedback will occur.

Social skills deficits may actually be large skills deficits that are seen most clearly in social situations. One ready example is sexual fantasy. If the client is struggling with appropriate expressions of their sexual fantasy, this will likely be apparent in other social situations. A similar argument may be made for the construct of self-esteem. A client with low self-esteem may lack the requisite social skills to adequately function, and addressing the self-esteem may be part and parcel with the social skills intervention. In these two examples, there are larger deficits that impact the social skills areas, and intervention should address both the larger issues, and the social skills needs.

Assessment and feedback will be given in the five following content areas: perception, interpretation, response generation, enactment and evaluation.

- *Perception*—is the client accurately perceiving the other party's intention? The client may perceive a blink as a wink, or an accidental touch as intentional.
- *Interpretation*—is the client making an accurate and appropriate interpretation of the other party's behavior? The client may take a smile as an invitation for physical contact, while the smiler had no such intention. Many males mistake female friendliness for sexual interest.
- *Response generation*—does the client have any deficits in their interpersonal repertoire? The client may only know two responses to a given stimulus, e.g., a smile. The client may respond in kind, or initiate physical contact, omitting options such as saying hello or making small talk. The client may have a limited fund of skills from which to draw upon, in this case, it is vital for the therapist to work with the client to identify alternative behaviors that could be employed.
- *Enactment*—is the client able to identify the appropriate response, but is unable to skillfully engage in the behavior? The client may know that it is appropriate to make small talk, but does not know how. In this case, the therapist will work with the client to practice implementing the skills at an appropriate level of skill.

- *Evaluation*—is the client able to accurately gauge the appropriateness and effectiveness of his performance. If a client is overly critical of their performance of appropriate behavior, they may be less likely to engage in that behavior in the future. Furthermore, if they are unduly positive in their self-appraisal, they may be misleading themselves into the likely consequences of such behavior. A videotaped interaction with a therapist confederate can provide rich data to be reviewed with the client for accuracy of evaluation.

While no published studies exist on the phenomena we describe below, it has been observed to play a role in several cases in which we have been called to lend our expertise. We have named this "Money in the Bank." The logic is as such: if one has built a long and reliable history of being socially appropriate, considerate and enjoyable at the workplace, one would be less likely to be reported for sexual harassment for a potentially reportable behavior or a "gray area" behavior. Likewise, we have encountered others who have, in part due to a near-complete lack of pro-social histories with their coworkers, were quickly reported for harassment for behaviors that were not reported on others. It has been our experience that the outgoing, appropriately-friendly, empathic worker who has shown consideration towards coworkers are less likely to be reported for the same behavior that may be reported for the worker is inconsiderate, ill-tempered or obnoxious. This speaks towards an intervention that the client can implement on a daily basis. By doing good deeds towards others, the client makes deposits in his social bank. Then, should he make a potentially sexually inappropriate comment, he would be forced to make a withdrawal. The hypothesis being that complaints are made only when withdrawals exceed deposits.

Eileen Gambrill (c.f., Gambrill, 1995a, 1995b) has described important components in social skills training. She's delineated 21 specific skill sets to be included in such an endeavor. The client should be encouraged to practice these skills in a safe and supportive environment, be that with therapist, friends, or loved ones.

1) Identify friendly people—Friendly people often:

    - Make eye contact
    - Smile at you
    - Use open gestures
    - Make conversation
    - Laugh

2) Offer friendly reactions—Friendly reactions are:

    - Making eye contact
    - Smiles

- Open gestures
- Head nods during conversation
- Complimenting others
- Listening attentively and actively

3) Greet people:

- Say, "hello" or "how are you" or "good morning"
- Shake hands

4) Initiate conversations:

- Talk about non-threatening, non-sexual subjects
- The weather
- Decorations
- Music
- Avoid personal questions initially

5) Introduce interesting topics (non-sexual and non-gendered):

- Observations
- Current events
- Movies, television, music, sports

6) Balance listening and talking:

- Listen to content of what is said
- Ask follow-up questions about what other says
- Relate your content to the other's content

7) Share information about yourself:

- Things you would feel comfortable with if everyone knew them
- Practice in advance in front of a mirror (though silly)
- Who you are
- What you do
- Where you're from
- What you like to do in your free time

8) Offer opinions:

- Be honest
- Be open to others having alternative opinions
- Your opinion may not be the "right" opinion
- There may not be a "right" opinion

9) Respond to criticism openly:

- Listen to the content
- Avoid being defensive

- It does show they care about you, if they didn't, they wouldn't say anything
- Admit to it if it is accurate
- Integrity and responsiveness to feedback builds respect

10) Share your feelings:

- Strike a balance between being open with everything and being closed off
- Discretion takes practice, both timing and content
- Others may follow your lead and express their feelings; be receptive

11) Change the topic of conversation:

- Change the direction of the conversation
- Appreciate the other's opinion, and ask for their thoughts on another topic
- Example, you seem to have good insights on things, what do you think about...

12) Disagree:

- State your opinion
- Allow others to state theirs
- Acknowledge the agreeable elements in their position
- Acknowledge the potential for a lack of agreement

13) Use humor appropriately:

- Toilet humor, sex humor, blonde jokes are off limits
- Funny observations and jokes are helpful

14) End conversations:

- Has two elements; compliment and departure
- Compliment: I appreciate what you've said; I've enjoyed our time together...
- Departure: Let's talk again soon, I'd like to talk about this later

15) Suggest activities to do together (if appropriate):

- If in sharing about yourself, they may share an interest in the same activity
- Suggest doing that activity together
- Fishing, shopping, antiquing can be done in groups, and may help develop relationships

16) Arrange follow-up:

- If you are interested in knowing the person better
- Ask about follow-up opportunities
- Coffee breaks or bagel breaks
- Lunch together, dinner together
- Sporting events

17) Request behavior changes:

- If you don't like what another is doing, tactfully request they change
- What it is
- Why it's bothersome
- What could be done instead
- If there is no change, you are free to leave

18) Ask favors:

- People like to feel helpful
- People don't like to feel taken advantage of
- Ask in a straightforward manner
- Don't beat around the bush
- Help others first, or ask if they can do you a favor
- Money in the bank helps you when you need to make a withdrawal

19) Respond directly to put-downs:

- Say, "I don't like what you just said."
- They can apologize or continue
- You can choose to stay or leave

20) Refuse unwanted sexual attention:

- Acknowledge your perception, "it seems like you're interested in me"
- Report your intention "I'm not interested in changing our relationship now"
- You can change the conversation, end the conversation, and leave.

21) Make appropriate overtures:

- Be honest
- Be direct
- If you sense resistance, let it go

- If they do appear interested, be oriented towards a mutually pleasing, safe, respectful experience

Useful Metaphors

Learning to drive—also learning to dance, or other similar activities

Learning to drive is a three-part process; instruction, observation and practice. Social skills are the same. Sometimes we get direct instruction, sometimes we get to watch others, and we need practice. Practicing ineffective or offensive social skills will not lead to improvement, just like practicing plane crashes does not lead to safe flying. Practicing effective and appropriate social skills leads to implementation of effective social skills. An important note is that while the person may recall and be able to demonstrate some of the skills without continued practice, people typically do better with continued practice and refreshers.

Schedule

20% Review
Praise client for successful completion of previous Denial & Minimization Module

20% Introduce Skills Training
Explain procedure
Describe and provide examples of errors and appropriate examples of perceptions, interpretations, response generation, enactments, and evaluations, (e.g., misread social skills, failure to engage in appropriate response, repertoire deficits).
Discuss boundaries and clear "don'ts"
Answer any questions

40% Discuss Skills Training
Role-play key interactions with client
Evaluate positives and negatives

20% Review
Review progress made during session
Outline next session's content and procedure

Dinner Customs

Ask the client to recall the first time they had dinner at a friend's house. Perhaps they were raised to say grace before dinner, and their friend was not. The client grew up learning from their parents about what to do and how to do it, just as the friend did. Yet when confronted with something different, the client saw an excess (saying grace) in their friend, or perhaps a deficit in themselves. An example from literature is seen in *To Kill A Mockingbird* when Scout reacts to her schoolmate's use of molasses at the meal.

Learning a Foreign Language

Sometimes social skills feel like a foreign language. Both are things others may be able to do, but for whatever reason, the client struggles. Both are learned, both take practice, and some are just plain tough. The key to this metaphor is validating the client's struggle with the issue, and hopefulness that things can improve.

Homework

Week one

- Role play social skills with friend or peer and solicit feedback
- Practice Gambrill's 21 away from work, with peers, friends and family
- Journal about experiences of Gambrill's 21

Week two

- Practice Gambrill's 21 at work
- Journal about experiences of Gambrill's 21 at work
- Solicit feedback from peers at work with whom client has practiced
- Sexual Harassment Myth Acceptance and Hostility Towards Women Scale for Module 5 to be completed before next session

Repeat or Proceed Decision Tree

1) If client demonstrates awareness of, and can engage in appropriate alternative behaviors for; perceptions, interpretations, response generation, enactments and evaluations, client should proceed to Module 4.
2) If the client is still demonstrating deficits in awareness and/or appropriate alternative responses in perceptions, interpretations, response generations, enactments and evaluations the client is to repeat the Module, focusing on buttressing the strong areas and addressing the weak areas.

3) It should be expected to spend between 2 to 4 sessions on social skills.

Therapy Transcript

T Well, it's clear that there's still some work to be done on minimization. My take on it is that we'll have lots of opportunities to practice—so if I see or hear you doing it, I'll try to call you on it right away.

R Sounds good.

T All right, what I'd like to move into next is a role-play.

R Make believe, seems odd, but you're the doc.

T Here's the thinking behind it—I want to see what you can do. It's sort of like practice before the big game. I want to see if you can tell the right play to run at the right time. Like if it's football, you need to see if the other team is going to blitz you and try to sack the quarterback, or if they're going to hang back. If they're running a blitz, you need to call for that, and make adjustments so your quarterback doesn't get sacked.

R Sounds good coach—what's the game plan?

T Nice job following the analogy, the plan is for you to pretend I'm a coworker, call me Steve, and we're chatting while we're waiting in line for the copy machine. I'm pretty new to the company. The person in front of us in line at the copier is another new hire; let's call her Maxine.

R All right.

T Hey Robert, how was the weekend?

R It was all right. How 'bout you—do anything fun?

T Yeah man, I got set up by a friend in accounting, went out to a comedy club.

R Oh yeah? Tell me about it.

T All right, hey Maxine—how long are we gonna have to wait?—Seems like Maxine had a second bowl of grump flakes for breakfast.

R (chuckles) hey man, what are you trying to do?

T I'm just saying she's a little wound up—maybe I should bust a few of those jokes I heard at the comedy club. That guy was hilarious. He told this one joke about how well if you're going to get lucky on a date within the first few minutes of the date and

R And this is while you had the date there?

T Yah, that's the best part, he was asking audience who was on a date, and like, half of clapped, and he's saying, ok—well, let me tell if you should bother paying for the next round...

R (chuckles again) All right, so I need to know, how can I tell if I'm going to get lucky

T All right, let's stop here for a second and review.

R Ok.

T Where are we?

R We're waiting in line at the copy machine.

T And?

R And you're telling me about your date.

T Any problems with this?

R Not really—not that I see.

T Ok, let's break down on five categories. First—perception, what did you perceive my intention to be?

R To chat about the weekend, pass the time until we got in on the copier.

T All right, and what did you interpret my actions to mean?

R Same thing sort of, that you felt it was ok to talk about this weekend stuff, and that you wanted to tell me what was going on.

T How about responses—how appropriate were your responses?

R Fine, the conversation kept going.

T And enactments—did you have any problems doing what you planned, for example, did you want to say something, and it didn't come out right?

R No, I pretty much said my piece.

T Ok... we need to go over a couple things. First, perceptions. Maxine could hear, and therefore was a party to this interaction. What did you perceive her intentions to be?

R I guessed she was just waiting to finish her copy job and move on.

T And your interpretations?

R Well, she didn't do much, so I guess she didn't mind.

T Responses—your responses worked to keep the conversation going. You egged Steve on, asked for more.

R So, I kept the conversation going, isn't that what I was supposed to do?

T You tell me, you're having a discussion of sexually themed matters in front of a coworker, who doesn't seem interested in the conversation.

R Oh. That's bad.

T Yup.

R Oh. Uhm ... maybe I should have said something like, hey Steve, let's catch up on that later.

T All right, anything else you would have said.

R Well ... uhm, I don't know.

T Would you want to keep the conversation going?

R Yeah.

T So what else could you talk about?

R I don't know, sports or work or something.

T Sure—put it into place—what would that look like?

R Uhm ... hey Steve, let's catch up on that later. How's the new project going?

T Sounds good. Maybe we can do another one, which might more closely resemble your trouble spots.

R Like you need help with your computer.

T Like I need help with my computer ...

MODULE 5: MYTH ACCEPTANCE, COGNITIVE DISTORTIONS AND NEGATIVE ATTITUDES TOWARDS WOMEN

Focus

This module will address the client's acceptance of myths, cognitive distortions and irrational attitudes and beliefs. Myths, cognitive distortions and irrational attitudes encompass the notion that a harasser's misperceptions allow them to behave in socially inappropriate ways. For example, a person who believes that women dress nicely to seduce men may be more likely to make inappropriate comments about a woman's appearance. Compare that to the person who believes women may dress nicely because they like the way they feel in that outfit. Thus, acceptance of myths, cognitive distortions and irrational attitudes establish a situation in which harassers feel more comfortable to act inappropriately.

Skills & Techniques

The first focus is teaching the client about sexual harassment. First, the client needs to know the variety of behaviors (including gender and sexual orientation) that can fall under the umbrella of questionable conduct. Second, the client (and perhaps the therapist as well) needs to be brought up to speed on the current legal issues concerning sexual harassment. For example, in the United States, the current legal standard is known as the "reasonable woman" standard. By this it is meant that the trier of fact must determine whether or not a reasonable women would find the behavior in question harassing. Thus, the client must know that their intentions do not make a behavior acceptable, but rather the court decides if the behavior is harassment. At the point the client should have already received a copy of the FAQs of Sexual Harassment. If the client does not still have ready access to their copy, provide another.

The second area, and related area is myth acceptance, and cognitive distortions. Your previous work in relapse prevention may serve as a guide in this area. For example, if the client is over-generalizing women's attitudes towards sex from a single experience, the client will be asked to search for information which will contradict their position. For example, the harasser may believe that women enjoy being groped at the workplace, and that a pinch on the buttocks is happily received by women. The harasser may think that women dress in a certain manner to "turn him on." The harasser may think that women who tell an occasional off-color joke are fair game for any lewd conduct.

Jenkins-Hall (1989) describes the steps for changing cognitive distortions in sexual offenders as: identification of the thoughts that lead to maladaptive behavior, analyzing the validity and utility of the thoughts, and an intervention designed to change the cognitive distortions into more adaptive cognitions. Jenkins-Hall details how McMullin's (1986) cognitive therapy approaches can be adapted to sexual offenders. We extend this application to sexual harassers.

1) *Provide alternative interpretations* such that the "client is taught that his initial interpretation of a given situation may not be the most accurate. [The client] is asked to generate a list of alternative explanations." (p. 210, Jenkins-Hall, 1989). Consider the example of the woman who copes with a co-worker's offensive and degrading jokes. The client would be asked to generate alternative explanations for why she might have laughed at the joke, such as hoping it would go away, hoping the client would stop on his own, or that maybe she felt pressure to tolerate it because she had seen coworkers ostracize the last person to complain about the client's jokes.

2) *Utilitarian counters.* In this move you ask the client to evaluate whether his thinking assisted or hindered the achievement of their desired outcome, e.g., did having a biased interpretation of the victim's behavior make it easier for you to justify your actions to yourself?

3) *Objective counters.* The therapist helps the client analyze the logic behind certain types of thinking, e.g., if a woman dresses sexily then it's ok for the client to pat her buttocks.

4) *Disputing and challenging*. These moves are based in Ellis's Rational Emotive Therapy. In this stage the client is asked to identify irrational types of thinking and beliefs, and these irrational statements and beliefs are challenged in therapy. For example, the belief that if a woman spends time on her appearance she wants sexual attention from men would be disputed for it's factually inaccuracy.

5) *Review client responses* on Sexual Harassment Myth Acceptance scale.

Handout #8 includes the following information for the client to track their experience of cognitive distortions. They are provided here as a list for you, and as a handout for your client.

- **Common Cognitive Distortions**—this is by no means a comprehensive list, and will look different from client to client, and within each client
- **Victim Blaming**—She led me on ...
- **Entitlement**—I deserve to ...
- **Minimizing**—It's not as bad as they said, all I did was...or, I'm not as bad as I used to be ...
- **Rationalizing**—All the guys do it, I was the one to be made example of ...
- **Projection**—The other person wanted what I wanted ...
- **Magnification**—She said she was interested in hearing about my new boat, and this shows that she was interested in me ...
- **Victim stance**—Here's another example of how they're out to make it tough for me ...
- **Catastrophizing**—I shouldn't even bother trying, there's no hope in me ever doing things differently ...
- **Overgeneralizing**—like catastrophizing and magnification, it's like the old saying goes—give an inch and they'll take a mile. Since she didn't report it the first time, she must not have minded any other time ...
- **All-or-nothing**—Like the above, seeing one's self or others in absolute terms leads one to be easily criticized or devalued and supports the abstinence violation effect, e.g., she's had sex with one of the coworkers, therefore she's "easy" or "a slut"
- **Negative bias**—Unrealistic perception of all events as negative, e.g., Even though I was complimented on my presentation, they didn't say anything nice about me ...
- **Positive bias**—Unrealistic perception of events as positive, e.g., Even though he said my presentation needed some more polish,

if that's the worst he could come up with, he must think it was fantastic...

- **Personalization**—inferring a personal meaning to non-personal events, e.g., She liked my presentation, so she must like me...

Useful Metaphors

House Built on Sand

In this metaphor, the client's behavior is described as the house, and the client's beliefs and cognitive distortions as the foundation built on sand. By being built upon such shaky foundations, the house will crumble and will not be safe for anyone.

The Angel and Devil

In this metaphor, the cognitive distortions are likened to the little devil that appears over the protagonist in the television shows, the devil encouraging the bad behavior, the gratifying response etc, while the angel is arguing for the more appropriate behavior. The client likely only hears the comments and encouragement set forth by the devil side, and may not

Schedule

20%	Review Go over last week's homework—any difficulties with social skills, any difficulties with Sexual Harassment Myth Acceptance scale pre-test, responses to be reviewed later in this session Praise client for successful completion of Social Skills Module
20%	Introduce Myth Acceptance, Cognitive Distortions, and Negative Attitudes Towards Women—explore, e.g., difference between sexy and aesthetically appealing versus sexual objects or "body partification" Explain procedure Answer any questions
40%	Discuss Module Review Sexual Harassment Myth Acceptance responses Discuss any accepted myths using the 4 techniques described above; alternative interpretations, utilitarian counters, objective counters, and disputes and challenges.
20%	Review Review progress made during session Outline next session's content and procedure

recognize alternatives. In this metaphor, the client is encouraged to identify the devil's contributions as offerings or suggestions, and not "real" things to be acted upon.

Bad Weather Report

In this metaphor, the cognitive distortions are described as a bad weather report. If the client were given a weather forecast that it was likely to be a cold and rainy day, he'd opt for warmer clothes, a jacket and umbrella. However, if in reality it were a sunny and warm day, they would be uncomfortable, overdressed, and likely embarrassed. The same happens when a client pays attention to the cognitive distortions. By attending to this misinformation, the client is not prepared for reality, and will likely not respond appropriately.

Homework

Week one

- Client should track the occurrence of the cognitive distortions, using Handout 8.
- Client to journal cognitive distortions observed in others to practice recognition of distortions. Journal should be directed towards the form of the distortion, the perceived function for the person making the distortion, and the impact on the client.

Week two

- Client is to practice identifying and modifying distortions as they occur at the workplace and at home.
- Client is to track the occurrences of the cognitive distortions using Handout 8.
- Client is to journal about their experience when noticing and modifying, as well as the apparent impact of this on others.

Repeat or Proceed Decision Tree

1) If client is demonstrating acceptance of Sexual Harassment Myths, Module is to be repeated. Client homework for repeated Module is the Sexual Harassment Myth Acceptance Scale.
2) If client is not accepting Sexual Harassment Myths, the client is to be progressed to Module 5.

Therapist Homework

Request supervisor report for workplace performance, reports of sexual harassment, and any observed positive changes, e.g., positive comments from colleagues, promotion, etc. Further, the supervisor should report any observed coping strategies, such as avoidance of high-risk situations, or successful management of high-risk situations.

Therapy Transcript

T Let's go over a few of your responses on the homework.

R Ok, how'd I do?

T I've a few concerns.

R Oh yeah? I thought I did great.

T Your answers suggest that you're not a, what's the phrase I saw on TV, a degenerate sexist pig. However, there were some things I'd like to review.

R Ok.

T "All people like to be told they are sexy, even at work."

R I think I put 2.

T Yes you did, 2 equals 'believe some' so you believe this to be somewhat true.

R Yah, true-ish.

T It's false.

R Really?

T Really.

R Ok, if you say so.

T Nope, not if I say so, tell me why people don't like to be told they are sexy, even at work.

R I thought people liked compliments.

T Is it a compliment?

R Yeah, I'm saying nice things. I mean, it's not like I'm say, hey Baby, nice hooters.

T That's a minimization.

R How so?

T Well, it's not as bad as whatever, so it's not really a problem.

R Oh, yeah. OK, so anyway, why can't I say a compliment at work?

T I didn't say that, I said, not all people like to be told that are sexy, even at work.

Robert's Sexual Harassment Myth Acceptance

Please rate the following statements according to this scale:

Believe Strongly	Believe Some	Neutral	Generally disbelieve	Disbelieve strongly
1	2	3	4	5

1. If an equally qualified man and woman applied for a position, the man should get the job 4
2. All people like to be told they are sexy, even at work 2
3. People who have a "reputation" around the office don't care if you make sexually explicit jokes in their presence. 2
4. Women are less rational than men are 3
5. Men are more capable of hard work than women 2
6. If someone owes their job to their boss, the boss is right to expect sexual attention or favors in return 4
7. No one can be forced to have sex if they don't really want to 5
8. Women are better in the home while men are better in the workplace 3
9. Men should be strong and always ready for sex 3
10. People secretly enjoy being hit on at work 1
11. You have to do and return favors to move up in the world 2
12. Sexual harassment is just people trying to get money from coworkers or companies they don't like 4
13. Women are the only objects of sexual harassment 2
14. People who smile a lot want sexual attention 2
15. Work is a good place to find sexual partners 2
16. People have a right to decorate their work area in any way they choose, even with sexy pictures 4
17. Blowing off steam by flirting and telling jokes of a sexual nature is natural and expected 2
18. Gay men are the only ones who harass other men 2

19. Women are flattered by sexual advances from men even when they fail to positively respond to these advances 2______
20. It is natural for men to be more aggressive when it comes to sexual relations with women 2______
21. Women are often inconsistent in terms of their non-verbal communications with men 2______
22. Women often mean "maybe" or even "yes" when they say "no" to sexual advances by men 2______
23. It is important for men to control the initial development of their relationships with women 3______
24. Women frequently use men to obtain status, security, or other things that they want 3______
25. Women who dress in a sexy manner at work are deliberately ending a message to men 2______
26. Highly attractive individuals (opposite sex for heterosexuals) "drive me crazy" and I sometimes do or say thing around them that I can't help 4______
27. Pregnant women use their condition to justify doing less work on many jobs in comparison to their coworkers 3______
28. Women are often flattered by sexual advances from their male coworkers 2______

R And I can't figure out why not.

T Well, you said it looks like a compliment, how does it work.

R Well, it would work to make them feel better about themselves.

T And how would it do that?

R They'd feel nice because someone noticed they looked nice today.

T So what's that focus of that comment?

R Their looks—that they're looking good.

T And do you go to work to look good?

R No, I go to work to ... oh.

T Go on.

R Well, I don't go to work to be told I look good, I mean I'm not a show pony.

T And how do you suppose it would make a coworker feel if you told her she looked sexy?

R Well, the comment is just that she looks sexy, and that's not her job. So, it probably wouldn't make her feel like a good worker. Might make her feel good if she wanted to be thought of as sexy though.

T You're distorting a little bit, and you're on to something.

R Ok, unless she's a stripper, or something, she's not going to work to be sexy. She's going to work, just like me, to earn some money, do something we like, and something I'm good at, and to spend time with people she likes.

T What's an alternative, or a replacement belief?

R That people like other compliments, you know, non-sexual compliments, like "nice job on that presentation!"

T Right on. Good job! Let's do another one. People secretly enjoy being hit on at work. One—Believe strongly.

R Yah, I put believe strongly.

T Care to change your answer?

R I suppose. I mean, all right, so I get that work isn't a place to be sexy and make hits on women, but how I am supposed to meet people I like, to have some fun?

T Good justification. Got anymore?

R Oh, come on. Seriously, how I am supposed to have fun at work. I mean, it's just a little harmless flirting.

T Let's break that one down, one at a time.

R How am I supposed to have fun at work?

T And?

R By talking with people, sharing stories.

T Appropriate stories that are respectful of the audience?

R Huh?

T When you tell stories, be sure not to irritate those listening.

R Ok, so I can have some fun at work. But still, what about harmless flirting?

T Is it harmless?

R Yah.

T How do you know?

R Well, for one I don't mean it to be harmful. And for two …

T Let's stop there. What's the road to hell paved with?

R Good intentions.

T How determines if something is harassing? The giver or the receiver?

R The receiver, and the courts.

T So how do you know if it's harmless?

R Well, if it were harmful, she'd report it.

T Would she? And even if she would, wouldn't it then be too late for you? You already have a record …

R Well, she might not, she might just let it slide, hope she could ignore it.

T Not so harmless.

R Well, what the hell I am supposed to do? Just stand there like a moron and not say anything?

T Any possible alternative subjects besides sex and innuendo?

R Can't think of any.

T Not a one?

R Nope.

T Huh. Guess you've never been to a movie, seen a television show, followed any interesting new stories, voted, read, been outdoors, been anywhere, been curious about anywhere, or have an interest in the lives of others. You may actually be the boringest man on earth.

R Now you're being ridiculous.

T Is the point made?

R Not really, I mean I wouldn't someone at work telling me I'm sexy.

T Men and women are different and even this might offend you in certain situations. Would you still feel comfortable if a gay man told you how yummy you looked, or if an unattractive woman was coming on to you?

R Yah, I hear you. Work isn't the place for sex, and there are lots of other things to talk about. And yah, I'd probably feel uncomfortable if Vince was hitting on me in front of people. I gotcha.

T And an alternative belief is ...

R People don't like being hit on at work?

T You got it.

MODULE 6: VICTIM EMPATHY

Focus

The focus of this section is to increase the client's empathy for past and potential victims. It has been argued that a lack of victim empathy may be one of the key setting factors in sexual harassment. Thus, increasing a client's ability to empathize with others may serve as one of the best inoculants against future incidents of sexual harassment. However, for the psychopath or sadist, this module may be contraindicated.

Skills & Techniques

Before diving into empathy work, the client first needs to understand empathy, and compassion. The first step is to work with the client to develop an accurate and useful definition of empathy. Distinctions can, and should be made for the related concepts of sympathy, pity, and compassion. Once the client has a definition of empathy, ask them to compare it to such things as sympathy and pity.

The client will be asked to watch a videotaped report of a victim's experiences with sexual harassment, taken from sexual harassment prevention materials (c.f., O'Donohue, 1997, please see www.mofz.com for more information). It is recommended that therapists only use materials with a demonstrated ability to increase empathy. The client will also generate a letter from the victim's point of view towards them. The therapist will ensure that the letter accurately reflects the issues and emotions from a victim's stance. The client will also be asked to write a sincere letter of apology to the victims, detailing awareness of the victim's emotional state. The client will not be required to mail this letter. The client will also be directed to write letters from the perspective as if they and their loved ones were victims of sexual harassment (Hall, 1995).

With the therapist, the client will be asked to imagine and discuss in detail how they would feel as a victim of sexual harassment. For this situation, that may benefit from role-playing situations in which (if applicable) they are:

- A gay man being victimized by a heterosexual
- An unattractive female
- An attractive female
- Their mother as a victim of sexual harassment
- Their wife, girlfriend, or daughter as the victim of sexual harassment

The letters and discussions should include all nine combinations of time (immediate, short-term and long-term) and consequences (self-esteem/affective experience, safety feelings, and work/career consequences).

As you may recall from earlier Module 2, Understanding Sexual Harassment, and the FAQs of sexual harassment, there are common emotional, financial, and interpersonal consequences for the victims of sexual harassment. These may include, but are not limited to, depression, anxiety, flashbacks, unusual fears, lack of trust, communication difficulties, nightmares, increased use of sick days, headaches, to name only a few. Victims of sexual harassment often describe, "feeling dirty." If they have a history of victimization, the sexual harassment may recall past abuse. Their may be feelings of guilt and self-blame. Victims often experience financial consequences; avoidance of work sometimes results in loss of job, or decrease in pay if they cannot use sick days.

Handout #6 is a victim empathy worksheet that may be useful in directing a client in this area. This worksheet can be used either all at once, or could be delivered piecemeal over the course of therapy to assess progress. Your previous work with empathy training can be of assistance in this area. Generally speaking, the client should be working towards viewing the impact of their behavior in increasing larger contextual frames. Or to put it another way, have the client draw a circle, like the inside of a tree, with themselves in the center, perhaps their family and loved ones in their next circle out, maybe friends in the next circle, church members and coworkers after that, and broader circles so that in the end, the circles could be extended to the country, world or universe. Empathy work seeks to expand the client's focus from just their center circle, to broader rings within their experience, then later towards imagining how they fit into another's circle.

Useful Metaphors

Air Traffic Control

A common metaphor for use in empathy is the radar metaphor. In this metaphor, the client's ability to perceive others is likened to faulty radar. If the client is air traffic control, and the other person is the airplane, if the client's radar is off, they will likely mislead the other, perhaps into a crash. By honing the radar, the client will be better able to locate the other and guide them safely to their destination. In this case, it is important to describe the benefit of *accurate* empathy.

The Submarine

A similar metaphor is the submarine without a periscope. The periscope allows the captain to see where the submarine is. If the periscope is broken, the captain might have to rely upon other sources of information, and these sources might not be as accurate.

The Thermometer

The client can be likened to a doctor without a thermometer. For the doctor, the thermometer helps the doctor assess the patient. Without a

Schedule

20%	Review Go over last week's homework Praise client for successful completion of Myth Acceptance, Cognitive Distortion, and Negative Attitudes Towards Women Module
25%	Introduce Victim Empathy Explain terms Answer any questions
35%	Discuss Module Discuss how client would feel as victim Discuss how client would feel if loved one were sexually harassed
20%	Review Review progress made during session Outline next session's content and procedure Review letters Repeat procedure

thermometer, the doctor is often left to rely upon the patient's self-report. While this report might be accurate, the thermometer helps the doctor make informed judgments and interventions.

Homework

Week one:

- Client writes letters described above 1) for each victim, a letter from the victim's perspective towards themselves, and 2) their letter of apology to the victim(s)

This module requires 2 sessions as a minimum. In second and following sessions, content should address letters and practice of empathic statements.

Week two:

- Client is to assess the emotional state of others while not at work, and later seek follow-up with that person. For example, while in conversation with family member, person should make a note of their perception of the other's mood, and then ask the person about their mood. Client should journal about the accuracy of their perceptions, and the impact of their query on the other person. This can be practiced several times per day, and the client's accuracy should improve over time. The client should be prepared for learning experience in which they are initially off-target, and may improve over time.

Week three:

- Client is to perform the above exercise, while at work, as appropriately as possible for the client and coworkers.

Repeat or Proceed Decision Tree

- Once the client has written the letters including all nine combinations of time (immediate, short-term and long-term) and consequences (self-esteem/affective experience, safety feelings, and work/career consequences) to a level of satisfaction, the client can proceed to the next module. For the very best client, this will take a minimum of two sessions. The therapist should request that the client return the letters at least 2 days before the next session. This adds a large response cost for the client, and may provide "grist for the mill."

Therapist Homework

- Review the letters from the victim perspective and the letters of apology. These letters may need grammatical and spelling corrections, as well as directions on content, plausibility, and thoroughness.
- Review the journaling of the empathy exercise in which the client assesses the veracity of their perception of others' moods, and the impact of his inquiries on them. Client should not be encouraged to engage in this homework at work until he has demonstrated success away from the workplace.

Therapy Transcript

T Let's spend some time reviewing the letter you wrote from the victim's perspective.

R Ok, this is the one for Cassie. She was a temp in our office in the fall of last year. With her what I did was, I was under her desk working on the hard drive for her workstation, and when I was coming up from the floor, I put my hand pretty high up on her thigh to steady myself. Check that, I didn't do it to steady myself, I did it to gratify myself, I could have used the desk, or chair or something.

T Nice catch.

R Thanks.

T Ok, so let's hear her letter.

R Robert. I am writing this letter to let you know the impact you have had on my life. It is very very difficult for a single mother like me to find a steady job that works with my needs. I don't have anyone to help me care for my child, so when I have a chance at turning a temp job into a permanent position, I really work hard to make that happen. But after what happened, because of you, I don't think I'll be working for this company any more. I don't feel safe or comfortable there. And there's more than that, I don't even feel like a person. You made me feel like a piece of trash. You made me feel like I was just a breathing version of some jerk-off magazine. I'm a person, dammit, and you took that away from me. What you did was perverted. You're a creep. What makes you think that's it's ok to look up my skirt and then grab my thigh. Even if I were some stripper or whore, like you seem to think I am, you need to treat me with respect. You had no right to do that to me, and there's nothing, not a thing you can do to give back what you've taken from me. I hate you, and I hate that there's probably more like you out there.

T That covers a lot of material. Let's go through the main points. I think you start off by writing about her background. Why did you do that?

R Well, I figured it wouldn't be ok to do if she had other resources, or things to fall back on. I mean, I didn't want to minimize it if I felt like she could afford to find another job. So I made up that part.

T All right, so you wanted to make it pretty tough on yourself. Ok. Then there were a couple more things, she doesn't feel safe, she doesn't feel comfortable, and she doesn't feel like a person. Start with feeling safe

R Well, she wouldn't feel safe if I was working there, because I'd victimized her. I'd made her into a sexual thing, and she couldn't trust me to not do that again. That goes along with the comfortable thing. I bet she'd be afraid of lecherous me lurking around each corner. I mean, I'm starting to feel like a real creep now. So yah, she couldn't feel safe or comfortable.

T And as for the feeling like a person?

R Well, that was the part about the jerk-off magazine too. What I did was basically use her for a cheap thrill.

T No basically about it. That's what you did.

R Ok, What I did was use her for a cheap thrill. I mean, she wasn't even a person to me at that point. She was there only for my sexual gratification—for my turn on. And yah, I did masturbate about that later.

T So why is that a problem?

R Uhm, well, it's not like she's there for that to happen. The girls that pose in those magazines know that's gonna happen, but she was just there trying to do her job. She's not there to fulfill my lonely fantasies.

T And what was next?

R Treating like trash, and the stripper comments were all about respect. And I didn't treat her with respect. I didn't give her what I demanded she give me. And that's not right.

T True. What else?

R I said that the next job probably wouldn't be any better. I don't know why I said that. Probably she's feeling hopeless. I know if I was her, and I couldn't find a job and stuff I'd be pretty down.

T Say that again.

R If I was her, and I couldn't find a job I'd be pretty down.

T Feel that.

R (tearfully) I am.

MODULE 7: RELAPSE PREVENTION, SEEMINGLY IRRELEVANT DECISIONS, POSITIVE ADDICTIONS, AND LIFESTYLE BALANCE

Focus

This module will reintroduce RP and outline the next few sessions. It should begin with an overview of RP, including a review of the terms, and the purpose of this intervention.

This module will present the concept of the seemingly irrelevant decision (SID). SIDs are those behaviors that might not lead directly to a high-risk situation, but are early in the pathway of decisions that place the harasser in a high-risk situation. For example, if the client reports that he is more likely to harass after drinking during lunch, a SID would be agreeing to attend a 2-martini luncheon with an attractive coworker. Thus module will also present the concepts of Lifestyle Balance and Positive Addictions.

Skills & Techniques

Begin by reviewing the offense chain, and work with the client to find examples within their experience. For the purpose of review, here is relevant information from earlier sections.

Offense Chain, Offense Cycle, and Offense Wheel

A pattern of behavior ranging from the non-offending (abstinent) through SIDs and setting the stage, High risk situation, PIG, lapse, relapse, AVE and return to abstinence. The sequence is variable both within and between harassers. For some, the PIG may occur between lapse and relapse, and for others it may occur before the lapse.

Work with the client to determine which decisions lead to high-risk situations. Coping skills are taught during this module. Once the client can identify high-risk situations and SIDs, the client will need to learn effective coping strategies. For example, the therapist can help the client to brainstorm strategies to prevent entering into a high-risk situation. The client may choose to walk away or the client may wish to change the situation so that the potential risk is lowered, e.g., moving a conversation to a room in which there are more people, more men, etc. The therapist should work with the client to ensure that client solutions and skills are

Abstinence – Non-Harassing – Faking normal

→ SIDs

→ Setting the Stage

→ High Risk Situation

→ PIG

→ Lapse

→ Relapse

→ AVE

→ Abstinence – Non-Harassing – faking Normal

Figure 5.1.

adequate and appropriate. The therapist may also role-play situations with the client to allow the client a chance to practice his or her skills in hypothetical high-risk situations.

Be sure to define how behaviors relate to one another in a probabilistic fashion. The key here is to influence this probabilistic stream of behavior.

Work with the client to present the concepts of Lifestyle Balance and Positive Addictions. As you may recall from earlier segments, one of the common elements of sexual misbehavior is that it often occurs under periods of stress. For example, stress may be a common element in your client's high-risk situations. In the Lifestyle Balance segment the therapist works with the client, generate methods to reduce stress, and more healthy ways to deal with stress when it occurs. One of these methods for stress-reduction has been described as *positive addictions*. By Positive Addictions, we mean those behaviors in which the client can engage during times of stress that are not harmful such as jogging, lifting weights, creative writing, sailing, or listening to music. It is important that the therapist use their clinical judgment to assist the client in finding an appropriate stress-reducing activity (see RP in daily life for more).

Recall the section on functional assessment earlier in this work. One aspect of that section was to inform the therapist as to the need being met by the harassment. We had the examples in which the same behavior (commenting on a bra) served three different purposes (escape from an unpleasant situation, awkward attempt to engage conversation, and titillation). Lifestyle balance addresses these unmet functions that may occur, should the client no longer engage in the behaviors that formerly worked in those situations. For example, should Lucas no longer be able to receive titillation at the workplace, that need for titillation may continue, though unmet. To help your client, you need to identify safe, legal, and healthy way to meet this need.

In this area, accurate assessment is vital. For the client having unmet emotional needs, this client may need supplemental therapy to address couples or family needs. For the client having unmet sexual needs, the client may need to develop an intervention in which titillation may be experienced at exotic dancing establishments, with adequate safeguards that keep the titillation contained to this environment. A potential danger here is that rather than act as a catharsis, viewing women in such an environment may lead the client to be further engrossed in his chain of deviancy.

Useful Metaphors

Choose Your Own Adventure

There were a series of books available many years ago that allowed the reader to make decisions at specific choice-points. For example, in one about a murder mystery, the reader may have been asked "do you choose to open the door to the basement?" or "do you choose to proceed down the hallway?" Based upon these decisions, the reader would either be attacked in the basement or discover an important clue down the hallway. While the outcomes of the small decisions can't be known in advance, this example highlights the variety of outcomes that can follow based upon a small decision.

Sliding Doors

This a fine film starring Gwenyth Paltrow in which the parallel outcomes of a woman's life are followed after her choice of one of two options. If you and the client have seen the movie, describe how there may similar situations in the client's life.

The Swimming Pool

This metaphor asks the client about where they can go swimming. The client will likely list a swimming pool, a river, lake, or pond. Ask the client if they could go swimming in the office. Unless your office has a rather large pool, this is unlikely. For the client to go swimming, they would need to do several things to increase the chances of swimming. Leaving the office, getting to pool, changing clothes, etc. Liken this to sexual harassment. For the client to sexually harass, they need to be in a place where sexual harassment could occur, be in a frame of mind where sexual harassment would be ok, etc.

Schedule	
10%	Review Praise client for successful completion of previous Empathy Module
20%	Introduce SIDs and Coping Skills Explain terms Answer any questions
50%	Discuss Module Preview High-risk Situations Discuss behavioral antecedents as SIDs Identification and generation of coping skills Discuss Positive Addictions
20%	Review Review progress made during session Outline next session's content and procedure

A Bear and His Honey

Describe a bear that enjoys honey, and seeks it out. Unfortunately for this bear, he has an allergy to bee stings. This bear has found honey in two places, one in the beehive, and one at the grocery store. Both are sources of honey available to the bear, one is free and will get him stung, and one will cost some money, but he has no chance of getting stung. The hive may be more appealing due to the "rush" and the cost of the store honey may prevent the bear from a night on the town with his bear buddies. The bear's continued good health depends on his forgoing the "rush" of facing death at the hive, and instead getting that need met elsewhere by getting his honey safely.

Homework

Week one

- Client to generate additional examples of coping skills
- Client to record instances of engaging in coping skills outside work

- Client to generate a Positive Addiction Plan
- Client to complete Self Report Sexual Harassment Inventory
- Client to prepare initial RP plan, defining lapses, relapses and SIDs, using Handouts 9 and 10 to help identify Offense Chain and Relapse Prevention Planning needs.

Session 2 of SIDs Module 6

- Review High-Risk Situations
- Review generation of coping skills, practice coping skills
- Review Positive Addiction Plan, review engagement in Positive Addiction Plan

Week two

- Client to implement and journal about new coping skills
- Client to implement a Positive Addition Plan
- Client to journal about experience of implementing Positive Addiction Plan, and review plan as needed.
- Client to improve initial RP plan, defining lapses, relapses and SIDs.
- This will become RP Plan, and will be an evolving document

Repeat or Proceed Decision Tree

In order to proceed to the next module, the client should be able to:

- Identify SIDs in their experience
- Identify mechanisms for identifying SIDs as they occur
- Identify and employ techniques for remediating SIDs as they occur
- Identify alternative coping skills
- Implement alternative coping skills
- Have a positive addiction plan
- Implement the positive addiction plan

Therapy Transcript

T Let's look through one of your examples and see if we can identify your SIDs.

R My SIDs, those are the little set-up moves.

T Right.

R Right. OK, which one?

T Pick one, pick one that's fresh in your memory and let's walk through it.

R Okeedokee—here's one where I almost found myself slipping last week.

T All right, so you're recognizing some problems already—good to hear, what's the example?

R Ok, so I'm checking my email, and I see that one of the new temps is having trouble getting her browser, uhm, her Internet, to load the pages she wants. I checked my schedule for the day and saw that I could get to her either within the next fifteen minutes, or at the very end of the day. I really wanted to check some scores on the web, and I didn't really want to go all the way to her area, and besides, there would be a lot of people there then, and not as many at the end of the day. I'd like if it weren't too distracting, so I opted for later in the day. I wrote her an email to see if she really needed it done right away, or if she could use another workstation for that, or do something else until 5. She wrote back and said she could wait, so I worked on another project until then. So, here I am at 5 o'clock, and we're supposed to check out at 5:30, so I toddle off to her corner of the cube farm, and find her still struggling with it. So, the cool thing I did was that I stood behind her, and asked her to replicate the problem in front of me, and when I saw what she was doing, rather than ask her to scoot over and have me lean over her to type things in and show her, I asked her to step out of her chair, and I took her chair and showed her. And, I didn't set it up so she had to lean over me or anything. Felt pretty cool, I must say. Doing the right thing.

T Right on. Sounds like that would have been a good chance for you to do your harassing thing, and you chose not to, and it worked out well for you.

R Yah. Pretty cool.

T But…

R Oh boy.

T Yup, there's a but. We were talking about the SIDs, the set-up moves that make you more likely than not to be in a danger zone later in the day. And you had a couple in this example.

R Really? Ok, like what?

T Well, she asked you to fix her problem, and when did you get to it?

R Later in the day.

T And why was that?

R Well, like I said, I wanted to check some scores, and

T Hold it there—did you need to do that then?

Robert's Relapse Prevention Plan

Offense Chain

When completing this worksheet, you may be directed to describe a single event that led to your participation in this intervention, your most recent event, a typical event, or the general theme across all instances of your sexually inappropriate behavior

I. Setting the Stage – where are you, what are you doing, how do you feel?

For me, setting the stage is usually because something happened with my wife. Where am I? After I leave home or on my way to work, I'll notice that I'm thinking about the money worries. What am I doing? I'm usually listening to 'aggressive' music – hard rock with lots of guitars and drums. Getting myself riled up. How do I feel? I feel discounted. That's it in a nutshell, when my wife seems to discount my contribution and I feel like I just don't matter.

II. Seemingly Unimportant Decisions (SIDs)

Seemingly Irrelevant/Unimportant Decisions (SIDS/SUDS): Decisions early in a behavior chain that place the client in a high-risk situation, e.g., the drinker deciding to get milk from the market near the liquor store rather than the market near day care center.

When I decide to do tasks asked of me. If I put things off until the end of the day, if I do the task when I know the person will be alone, when I decide to 'do to by myself' and not have a back up or assistant.

III. Risky Situation

High Risk Situation: A situation identified by client and therapist as one in which the client has a greater likelihood to experience a lapse or relapse. Part of a behavior chain that probabilistically could lead to a lapse or relapse.

Anytime I'm alone with a young and attractive worker, especially if she's a temp. Making it even worse, if I'm feeling discounted or frustrated, and I have to go under the desk to get access to her workstation.

IV. Lapse

Lapse: An occurrence of an undesired behavior in the context of behavior cessation or reduction program (e.g., smoking a cigarette by the client in a smoking cessation program or visiting a bar by an alcoholic). A lapse is always less serious than a relapse.

Being around a young temp without backup or other people present. Not having others around to add a firewall for my own problems. ANYTIME I go under a desk to get access to the computer. Thinking about previous times when I've harassed, masturbating to those fantasies. Fantasizing about co-workers. Using sexually explicit materials and imagining the models as co-workers. Thinking I don't need help, or that it's all under control.

V. Abstinence Violation Effect (AVE)

Abstinence Violation Effect (AVE): The AVE occurs when a client lapses and irrationally concludes that the lapse is so severe, that they may as well relapse (e.g., since I broke the rule and I had one shot of whiskey, I may as well finish the bottle); a form of perfectionist or "all or none" thinking.

Giving up - I haven't done this one yet, so I can guess as to what it will look like. I guess just giving up, thinking that there's no turning back. If I'm already busted, I'd probably think that I may as well get my money's worth. Instead, I need to check myself and remind myself that I can stop at anytime, and the soon I stop it, the better I make it for myself, and my family, and for my victim.

VI. Relapse

Relapse: A violation of the contract or terms of the behavior cessation or reduction program. Sometimes defined as a return to pretreatment levels of the problem behavior.

Any physical contact with a female coworker. Leaning over the keyboard or her workstation and touching her breasts, actually any part of her, with any part of me. Using the excuse of 'balance' or 'getting up' to touch her legs. Doing the other stuff in my lapses.

Notes

This is only a rough draft. I need to work on revising this pre-test. The sophisticated plan includes my dynamic risk factors as well as static. The sophisticated plan applies to new situations, it has my stuff in the abstract. Work on this!!

R No.

T Ok, so you wanted to check the scores and ...

R And there are a lot of people in her area and it'd be easier at the end of the day.

T Let me translate that from harasser-speak into real language—you wanted her to be alone and without many witnesses, so you used checking scores on the web to set up a situation for you.

R Hey now ...

T Yes?

R Well, I mean it's not like that—I wasn't trying to set her up like that

T It might not have been a well-thought decision, that's why we call them "seemingly irrelevant ..."

R It's not like I was stalking her.

T Thank you sir, may I have another. Come on now; look at how that little decision set both her and you up for a danger zone, for a high-risk situation.

R I suppose you're right. It's not like that's what was on my mind, but it sure worked that way.

T I like that way of looking at it—how it worked. In this case, you're right, that decision to check the web for sports scores worked to set up a high-risk situation for you.

R Seeing these takes practices, let's find a few more ...

MODULE 8: HIGH-RISK SITUATIONS

Focus

This module will focus on an ideographic assessment of high-risk situations. High-risk situations are those situations in which the problem behavior is most likely to occur. If the problem behavior is the telling of crude jokes, the client may only be at risk for joke telling in the break room, or in the break room when only three or more male coworkers are present. Again, this speaks to the need for a comprehensive and detailed assessment. If the problem behavior is frottuerism or inappropriate touching, high-risk situations might include being in the elevator, or in the copy room. There is no clear-cut criterion for what constitutes a high-risk situation, but your previous work in RP can help in the identification of high-risk situations.

Skills & Techniques

The client and clinician will work together to identify the situations in which the client has previously harassed and those situations in which he is likely to harass. The client will be directed to write the antecedents of each sexual harassment incident (reported and unreported), and their corresponding sexual harassment behavior. If possible the client will be asked to report on any pre-disposing emotional, physiological, or environmental states that were present during their incidents of sexually harassing behaviors. If the client has difficulty generating examples, the therapist is to use each incident listed in the supervisor and/or investigator report.

Before a client can respond *to or* avoid *a High Risk Situation, the client must first be able to* recognize *a High Risk Situation*

In actuarial prediction measures for sexual offending and violence prediction, static and dynamic risk factors are included. For the sexual harasser, the same concerns apply to their identification of high-risk situations. Dynamic factors are changing, malleable elements that can be addressed and intervened upon directly. One dynamic factor often included is participation in treatment. This holds for the clients found to have sexually harassed. Our experience is that act of being in treatment typically lower their risk for later sexual harassment. Other dynamic elements can be mood disorders or other psychological problems. There are some elements that are not malleable, and therefore considered static risk factors. In sexual offending, the age at first offense is an unchangeable risk factor. For the sexual harasser, the presence of petite redheads may be an unchangeable risk factor.

Example: Thursday October 28, 2001, 3 p.m. I was a little stressed after 1 o'clock meeting with my boss. She was unhappy with the report I had submitted. I had written what I thought was an accurate report, and it reflected poorly on another co-worker. Anyway, the boss didn't really tear into me, but I got the point that she was unhappy with that particular piece of work product. I went back to my cubicle and was checking my e-mail when I got a funny e-mail from an old college buddy. It was this funny blonde joke. So I saw a coworker who I knew would like the joke over by the copy machine. I went over to the copy machine and started telling Tim the joke. It was a funny joke, but since the punch line involved something about a blonde with big breasts, one of the other co-workers got upset. I was just having a bad afternoon, and thought telling the joke would help me lighten up.

The client will be asked to generate a list of situations that are low-risk, and what aspects of those situations differentiate them from high-risk situations. The focus will be to train the client to recognize themes and commonalties in their high-risk situations so that they can generalize the ability to assess level of risk in a novel situation. The therapist will work with the client to ensure that the client is realistic in their assessment of the level of risk in a variety of hypothetical situations. For example, the therapist will create a series of hypothetical situations, based on the client's self-report of risk factors, to assess the client's ability to determine the causes and severity of risk.

Let's take the hypothetical example of a corporate CEO named Paul. Paul has risen through the ranks of his corporation, first a vice-president in charge of his state, and now CEO of the operation. He is now seeking treatment because it came to light that he has, on at least ten occasions, unexpectedly touched a 21 year-old intern. And while Paul never made any explicit sex-for-promotion demands, the intern felt obligated to tolerate the behavior. Paul reports that he only engaged in this behavior while he was at work in his private office. In asking Paul about the specifics of each encounter, it is learned that Paul only engaged in this behavior 1) with young interns, 2) on weekends and evenings, 3) under periods of stress, and 4) when privacy could be assured by using the study off the main office.

As a therapist you would work with Paul to predict when these situations may arise and to appropriately acknowledge the situations when they do occur. With Paul, you would work to identify solutions to being alone with young interns, for example, instituting an intern-buddy system, making sure that doors were left open whenever an intern was present, arranging the environment such that interns stayed to one side of the office while Paul was on the other side of the office. Although the lifestyle balance section will address the relationship between stress and problem behavior, it is important for both you and client to realize its importance in the high-risk situations.

Useful Metaphors

The Shoplifter

Where is the shoplifter most likely to get into trouble? In crowded shopping malls with tight security. That's the obvious answer, a physical location. The shoplifter is also likely to get into trouble when they are in a stressed out mood, or needing a "rush," an emotional location. Habitual shoplifters liken the experience to skydiving, there's a thrill in doing it, and a rush when they pull it off. If they are feeling the need for a rush, they are walking, talking high-risk situations. In this case, we've often likened the high-risk situation as being in the size 9 (or whatever the client's size) loafers at the end of the client's ankles. Wherever the shoes go, that's where the high-risk situations goes.

The Pedophile

The metaphor has the potential to alienate the client, so it must be used with caution and discretion. In this metaphor, ask the client to identify where pedophiles might go if they wanted to find a victim. Relate each of those areas to risk. Are they high-risk or low-risk? Most likely, places or jobs where the pedophile would be in contact with children would be considered high-risk, playgrounds, schools, child-oriented restaurants etc. would be considered high-risk, and places like cemeteries and record stores generally lower-risk.

Schedule

20% Review

Discuss last week's homework, the SRSHI. Look for examples of new disclosures made through the questionnaire that have not been presented in therapy, look for any denials and/or minimizations (in comparison with the record)

Praise client for successful completion of denial and minimization

30% Introduce the concept of High-Risk Situations

Explain procedure

Clarify expectation of client participation in treatment

Answer any questions

30% Discuss High-Risk Situations

Client describes antecedents and behaviors for each instance of sexually harassing behaviors

Client and therapist work together to identify distinguishing features of high-risk and low-risk situations. Client and therapist work together to generate avoidance and coping skills for high-risk situations, e.g., not being alone in copy room, increased self-monitoring, and rules related to these situations.

Continue in next session if more time is necessary

20% Review

Review progress made during session

Outline next session's content and procedure (either a continuation of high-risk or outcome expectancies)

The Redhead

In this metaphor, liken the client to a redhead living in Arizona. Typically redheads don't fare to well in heat and sunshine, so if they were to live in such an environment as Arizona, they would need to take protective measures to safeguard their health. Such measures taken to mitigate the dangers of sun and heat can be likened to a relapse prevention plan. For example, staying indoors, use of hats and sunscreen, air conditioning and all things that can be done to help tolerate the situation, while moving to Seattle might be an environmental alternative.

Homework

Week one

- Client to identify their high-risk situations
- Client to generate a list of means to avoid/escape/manage high-risk situations
- Client to journal about experiences of being in high-risk situations
- Client to implement escape/avoidance/management strategies of high-risk situations away from the workplace
- Client to improve their Relapse Prevention plan from previous module

Week two

- Client to implement escape/avoidance/management strategies at the workplace
- Client to journal about experiences of implementing strategies in high-risk situations
- Client to improve Relapse Prevention plan to include high-risk situations

Repeat or Proceed Decision Tree

1) If the client has identified high-risk situations and psychological, physiological, and cognitive antecedents, as well as generated reasonable and manageable avoidance and coping skills, client is ready to begin next module.
2) If the client has not identified high-risk situations, antecedents, or generated reasonable and manageable avoidance and coping skills, the client is to repeat module.

My Relapse Prevention Plan

Worksheet

Emergency Numbers

Therapist Dr. O'Donohue, (775) 555-1869

Peer Support Wife!, if she's not there, Dave P, (626) 555-1942, Chris M, (303) 555-5309, Catherine F, (360) 555 3344

Human Resources Contact Joan B, (206) 555-1789 ext 1300, if not in, Pat A., (206) 555-1789, ext 1350

Definitions:

What my lapses look like Being around young attractive female (temporary) coworkers, after STAGE IS SET and in HIGH RISK. Being under desk at work, being alone at work, doing work in isolated (non-public) areas. Fantasizing about previous harassment or coworkers. Using sexually explicit materials to feed fantasies of sexual activity at work.

What my relapses look like Any physical contact with coworker, leaning over the keyboard, using excuse of 'balance' or 'getting up' Doing the stuff in lapses in conjunction with each other, or with this stuff.

What to do when I lapse (or recognize that I've lapsed) After I recognize, I need to respond to it - that means get out of the situation with minimal damage, acknowledge it to the other person or people, and then report it to my therapist and support group.

What to do when I relapse (or recognize that I've relapsed) Same thing as when I lapse - recognize, respond and report.

III. Risky Situation

High Risk Situation: A situation identified by client and therapist as one in which the client has a greater likelihood to experience a lapse or relapse. Part of a behavior chain that probabilistically could lead to a lapse or relapse.

Anytime I'm alone with a young and attractive worker, especially if she's a temp. Making it even worse, if I'm feeling discounted or frustrated, and I have to go under the desk to get access to her workstation.

IV. Lapse

Lapse: An occurrence of an undesired behavior in the context of behavior cessation or reduction program (e.g., smoking a cigarette by the client in a smoking cessation program or visiting a bar by an alcoholic). A lapse is always less serious than a relapse.

Being around a young temp without backup or other people present. Not having others around to add a firewall for my own problems. ANYTIME I go under a desk to get access to the computer. Thinking about previous times when I've harassed, masturbating to those fantasies. Fantasizing about co-workers. Using sexually explicit materials and imagining the models as co-workers. Thinking I don't need help, or that it's all under control.

What does my AVE look like? Like I said, Catastrophizing - giving up. When I get depressed and down on myself, and then I lapse - wow, I could be in real trouble of going down relapse AVE.

Other Issues

Chemical Dependency Thankfully for me, not an issue. But it could be. I need to be on the lookout for this, because if I'm not dealing with the things that lead me to do this harassment in the first place, I might turn to booze. Keep an eye out for this one.

Comorbid concerns

Anxiety Money worries are the big anxiety things. When I get worried about money, that has been a stage-setting event for me before. Also worries about my wife and baby too.

Depression Dealing with this stuff gets me depressed, and if I'm depressed, I'm likely to give up, and if I give up, then I relapse, and if I relapse I may go down the AVE, and if I go down the AVE I may as well give up altogether. That's what depression does to me. Now that looks like victim stance, the victim of my depression. I need to get treatment for the depression too if it's getting in the way of my not harassing. I need to follow-up with my therapist or get a new therapist for this.

Personality Disorder We haven't really gotten into this one. My therapist said it might be an issue to improve aftercare.

My Relationship This is the big one. Problems with my wife often leave me feeling unimportant, and that has set up all this it seems. So when I don't do what I need to do manage those feelings and emotions, I set myself up to get into trouble and hurt someone. I need to work with my spouse, and maybe get counseling together to improve our relationship, and work with my therapist to improve how I manage my feelings as a husband and father.

My Spirituality For one, I need to talk with my minister about this. She could help. When I revise my plan, I should have her name on the support list, and to have disclosed to her.

My Relapse Prevention Plan

Worksheet

How tos:

1) How to avoid High Risk Situations/lapse/relapse First step is recognition. I need to review these at the start of each workday. Every day I'll check this list. I'll talk with two of my support staff and let them know that at times I'll want them as back-up, even it seems a simple task. I'll reserve the first and last hours of the workday to work in my office, checking email and stuff. I'll provide weekly check-ins to my HR person, and continue to meet with my therapist.

2) How to cope in High Risk Situations/lapse/relapse If I can't avoid it, I need to have a back up. I need to ask the woman to step away from the workstation. I need to not go under the desk if there's someone there. I need to take this piece of paper out of my pocket and read it. I CAN ALWAYS LEAVE AND COME BACK LATER. HR SAID THEY'D PREFER ME TO DO THIS THAN TO HARASS.

3) How to escape High Risk Situations/lapse/relapse When I do this, I just say to them that I need to return to my office, and direct them to a back-up computer. I then call the HR person, and contact my staff support and ask them to handle it. Then I leave a voice mail with my therapist. It's not just walking away, it's

walking away without hurting anyone, and taking steps to keep myself safe.

4) How to re-group after a High Risk Situation/lapse/relapse Debrief with my HR person and therapist at next session. Ask HR person and support staff to see if there were any problems with follow-up for the person's problems. Journal about it. My thoughts feelings, emotions and behaviors before, during and after.

Therapy Transcript

T Ok, we've already talked a good deal about some of these things, these risky situations.

R Yah.

T And you see some of the challenge of trying to present this information in pieces, because we need to, in a sense, set up the high risk situations by laying the foundation with SIDs and the offense cycle.

R Gotcha—sort of like we covered the prelims and now we're covering the important stuff.

T Let me check you on that—all of this stuff is important. The SIDs are things that can set-up the high-risk. Usually the high-risk situations will be obvious, and easy to see. The SIDs

R (interrupts) are sneaky little buggers.

T Right, the SIDs are sometimes tougher to find.

R Ok, so high risk—those are ...

T Those are the situations in which we would say you would be tempted to, or perhaps you're more likely than not to sexually harass.

R Ok, I know a couple of easy ones—and we've, like you've said, we've talked about these in general already.

T Ok, so what are they?

R All right, uhm, well, pretty much any time there's a temp worker—coz they don't know my style, who has, uhm, computer trouble and needs my help.

T What else about those situations?

R Well, the setting the stage stuff would be if I was having trouble at home. But say I need to get under the desk to access the workstation, or if there's any opportunity for physical contact. I could rub on her or up against her—what was the word for it?

T Frottuerism?

R Yah, frottage. Uhm, guys aren't high risk, regular workers aren't high risk, late in the day tends to be more high risk than others, but sometimes I'm more of an opportunitist.

T Nice insight—what else?

R Nothing about physical traits—except for large, uhm, breasts.

T That's what they're called—so if the woman has large breasts you may be more inclined to rub against her?

R Yah, that's true.

T And if she's a temp, and you need to work under her desk, while she's there?

R True, true and true.

T And I don't want this to seem like we're blaming the women here—we're finding features that you look for, warning signs. These women are, well, let me turn it to you, what are these women doing at work?

R They're there to make a living, have a career, feed their family, provide for themselves, and maybe enjoy themselves. They're not there for me. I learned that lesson.

T Right, so if they look nice, or are wearing perfume, that's ...?

R That's not for my benefit.

T Nice. Ok so, let's say you're in this high-risk situation, this danger zone ... what do you do?

R I leave.

T Is that always reasonable? That can be a good strategy to use most of the time, but what if you can't really do that. What's another option?

R No, I mean, you're right, I can't always do that—part of my job is to be under the desk, tooling around on the workstations checking the cables, unhooking and installing their machines, things like that.

T Right, so what to do instead.

R I guess I need to figure out how to manage those situations. Sort of like the alcoholic who has to go to parties as part of the job.

T Yah, good point. Let's talk about that a bit more. Coping strategies are an important component of high-risk situations. When we talk about lapses, we talk about not using your relapse plan when you're in a high-risk situation. Before we get to that, let's review all of your disclosed events so we can see if there are any other elements in common that make for high risk situations ...

MODULE 9: OUTCOME EXPECTANCIES AND THE PROBLEM OF IMMEDIATE GRATIFICATION

Focus

The ninth module will address outcome expectancies and the problem of immediate gratification (PIG, Marlatt, 1989). In this population, the outcome expectancies are the client's beliefs about the likelihood of a given outcome. For example the client may believe that the likelihood of a woman being offended by his behavior is low, say 1 woman in 20 would be bothered by his behavior. Another relevant outcome expectancy may be the client's belief in the likelihood of actually experiencing adverse consequences due to his sexual harassment. The client may feel that his behavior may result in, at most, a talking to by his boss. Thus, the goal of this segment of therapy is to make the client's outcome expectancies more realistic.

An additional focus in this area is the problem of immediate gratification, the PIG. In essence the PIG is an undue focus on the short-term consequences in the face of perhaps more severe long-term consequences. The relationship between outcome expectancies and the PIG are clear, the needs to be aware of both short and long term consequences for both appropriate and inappropriate behavior.

Skills & Techniques

The therapist will use psychoeducational approaches to teach the client how to create a decision matrix. The matrix will contain the positive and negative outcome expectancies for harassing and not harassing, in both the immediate and long term. The therapist will challenge any unrealistic outcome expectancies until the client is able to generate more realistic outcomes. On the next two pages, you can see an example worksheet for Outcome Expectancies. In the context of outcome expectancies, the PIG should be discussed. The client can be asked to analyze past situations in which they harassed, and to compare the immediate gratifications against the long-term consequences.

Given this client's responses, you would want to address the following responses and outcome expectancies:

1) What is the likelihood of each of the listed short-term positive consequences? Is it realistic to expect that Susan would find this flattering? Assign a probability (.00 to 1.00) to each of the outcomes. Discuss how realistic the probability is given the client's statement.
2) What is the likelihood of each of the listed long-term positive consequences? Is it realistic to expect that Susan would like to pursue a long-term relationship with the client? Assign a probability (.00 to 1.00) to each of the outcomes. Discuss how realistic the probability is given the client's statement.
3) What are some more realistic short-term negative consequences? For example, Susan might feel embarrassed, afraid, ashamed, humiliated and disgusted. Assign a probability (.00 to 1.00) to each of the outcomes. Discuss how realistic the probability is given the client's statement.

Emphasize that his probabilities occur in a context in which he has a history of sexual harassment

---

Example Decision Matrix

Describe the Harassing Behavior or Situation: I'm in the copy room with Susan. She's looking really good today, and I can tell by the way she's looking at me, that she is interested in me. So I go up to her, put my arm around her waist and say, "Wow Susan, you look really good in that dress, it really shows off your figure! I bet you get lots of attention when you go out dancing... speaking of which, I heard there's a new club opening up downtown, how'd you like go down there this weekend and try it out?

List the short-term positive consequences of harassing:

1. She'll laugh and giggle
2. She'll agree to go to the club with me
3. I might get to have sex with her this weekend

List the long-term positive consequences of harassing:

1. I might end up going out with Susan
2. I might end up meeting a girl at the club
3. Susan will appreciate my initiative in asking her out

List the short-term negative consequences of harassing:

1. She could say no
2. I wouldn't get to go dancing this weekend
3. She could really bust my balls and say I sexually harassed her

List the long-term negative consequences of harassing:

1. I'd lose my job if Susan thinks I harassed her
2. My wife would be upset that I lost another job or got transferred again
3. I might not get together with Susan

List the short-term negative consequences of not harassing.

1. I wouldn't get to feel that 'rush' when I can make women embarrassed.

2. I wouldn't get to see if she liked me.

3. I'd still be all stressed-out.

4. I know I won't get to have sex with Susan.

List the long-term negative consequences of not harassing.

1. We might not ever get together.

2. She'd think I was a wimp for not taking the initiative.

3. The guys would razz me for not taking advantage of the situation

List the short-term positive consequences of not harassing:

1. I guess she wouldn't feel awkward.

2. I wouldn't have to catch any guff from my boss.

3. She wouldn't call in HR on me.

List the long-term positive consequences of not harassing:

1. She might respect my professionalism

2. I'd keep my job

3. It would probably be a nicer place to work.

4) What are some more realistic long-term negative consequences? For example, rather than focusing on the negative consequences to his sex life with his co-workers, this client should focus on negative outcomes for the victims (like those presented in (3) above), and for himself, e.g., loss of income, inability to pay for child's college, and the shame his wife and children would experience were knowledge of this incident made public. Assign a probability (.00 to 1.00) to each of the outcomes. Discuss how realistic the probability is given the client's statement.
5) Compare the long-term consequences against the short-term consequences. Do the short-term positive consequences seem more salient to the client than the long-term negative consequences? Work with the client to identify which aspects of the short-term consequences are important, and which of the long-term consequences are aversive.

Useful Metaphors

The Gambler's Fallacy

This metaphor is taken from the standard statistics text. The gambler's fallacy is the gambler's notion of being "due" if they've had a recent string of losses. Even if the last ten roulette spins have resulted in red, the odds of black coming up next are still 18:38. The previous outcomes have no bearing on the next spin, as the ball and wheel don't remember what

Schedule	
10%	Review Praise client for successful completion of High Risk Situations Module
20%	Introduce Outcome Expectancies and the Problem of Immediate Gratification Explain terms and procedures Answer any questions
50%	Discuss Module Review Example of Decision Matrix Have client work through blank Decision Matrix
20%	Review Review progress made during session Outline next session's content and procedure

happened before. The gambler's cognitive distortion leads the client to misperceive the likelihood of possible outcomes.

The Eeyore Experience

Eeyore, from Milne's *Winnie the Pooh* stories is known for attending only to the negative elements in his experience. Eeyore also has a knack for only predicting negative outcomes for future events. Ask the client to imagine living in Eeyore's world, see if they can recognize missing elements. You may even take this a step further, and ask them to role-play Eeyore to highlight the drawback of having exclusively negative outcome expectancies.

The Pollyanna Principle

Like Eeyore, Pollyanna is known for attending to only half of the possible outcomes, though in her experience, only the unusually positive possible outcomes. The client may benefit from presenting both metaphors and highlighting the benefit of living a synthesis of Eeyore and Pollyanna.

This module requires at least two sessions. In second and following sessions, content should address decision matrix difficulties and reasonableness.

Homework

Week one

- Client to complete Decision Matrices for each victim and/or type of sexual harassment in his offense record
- Client is to complete Decision Matrices for any instances of sexual harassment he views himself as vulnerable to commit
- Client to implement Relapse Prevention plan
- Client to journal about Relapse Prevention plan
- Client to modify Relapse Prevention plan

Week two

- Client to review outcome matrices accuracy with feedback from peers
- Client to implement Relapse Prevention plan
- Client to journal about Relapse Prevention plan
- Client to modify Relapse Prevention plan

Repeat or Proceed Decision Tree

If the client is able to realistically complete a week's worth of decision matrices, the client is ready to proceed to the next module.

Therapy Transcript

T You mentioned earlier that you were having some difficulties at home and that these were getting in the way of your progress.

R Yah, that's about it. I mean, I can't seem to let go of the problems at home, so I end up taking 'em to work, and then I end up taking it out on my coworkers. I get snappy and stuff.

T What else about that?

R Well, uhm, I'm not doing as good of work as usual. I don't think anyone really notices, and it's only been happening for a while.

T Ok, but the point is that you're hanging on to your stress at home and taking it to work.

R Yah.

T So what do you do to get rid of stress?

R (chuckles) Well, before this I'd cop a feel.

T Uh-huh. And now that that's off the table.

R That's the, pardon the pun, the rub.

T Yup. So where do we go from here?

R I need something to do, to make the stress go away.

T You want to do something about it—something to make the problem go away, and you want that to happen A S A P?

R Roger.

T All right, and you want that problem addressed immediately.

R Yes.

T And before, what you'd do to feel better is to act on the impulse right away, get the instant feel good, and worry about damage control later.

R Yah, and now I'm stuck. And I'm not a big drinker, so I can't do that, so sometimes when I'm needing a little boost, I'll check some porn sites at work. And since I'm the I.T. guy, I can get away with it.

T So now, the immediate gratification is not getting the rub, but checking out some porn at work.

R Yah.

T And would that be a problem, were your bosses to know?

R Yah, we've got a pretty strict no-porn policy. We let folks do some personal web stuff at work, like booking flights, and shopping on breaks and stuff. But we do check the sites, and we can tell if it's a raunchy site, so, yah, I'd get busted. And given my troubles, probably be bounced out.

T All right, so this sets up what we call the PIG, and feeding the PIG.

R The pig?

T PIG: Problem of Immediate Gratification.

R The instant feel good to make it better?

T Just so. What do you suppose happens when you feed the PIG?

R Feed the pig—well, I suppose it'd feel better right away, and it'd likely be hungry again later.

T The analogy works pretty well. The science behind it is something like this—if you're motivated mainly by avoiding the unpleasant experience you're having *right now*, you're less likely to pay attention to the far off consequences you're likely to face later on.

R Like the opposite of 'a stitch in time saves nine?'

T Yah, by acting under the 'right now' problem you often neglect the 'down the road' problems.

R Heh, yah. I can see this one with food. I can never pass up a good chiliburger, but my gut hates me about 3 hours afterwards. And that saying—a moment on the lips and forever on the hips.

T Yes. And it's not like we're breaking new ground here with this psychology stuff. This all stuff we've known about for a long long time. The job here is just to present the problems you're having around these issues. The PIG fits in with over eating, drinking, drug abuse, and yes, sexual misbehavior. What are some areas in which you don't feed the PIG?

R Well, about the only one I can think of is with music. I'll usually wait until a CD I like is on sale before I buy it.

T How do manage to succeed with that? You don't rush out and buy it right away...

R No, no I don't. I tell myself that I can wait, and that it'll be on the radio. That and the fact that I know someone else will buy it and it'll show up at the used music store before too long. I don't know how that's similar to what I'm dealing with here, so what do we do about it?

T It sounds like you've identified some components of that situation that make it easier to avoid the PIG. Now what we try to do is have you work through some exercises so that it's easier for you to look at the long-term outcomes more quickly when faced with a PIG situation.

R All right, that sounds like a good plan. Let's try it.

T (getting hand out ready) This worksheet is on Outcome Expectancies. The PIG relates to outcome expectancies in that if you don't expect negative outcomes, you're going to be biased into feeding the PIG. So step one is to outline the expectancies, see if you're out of line on what you see a potential outcomes, and then we'll work from there.

R Ok, let's see this worksheet.

MODULE 10: REVIEW AND INTRODUCTION TO RP IN DAILY LIFE

Focus

The tenth module will review the previous modules, assessing client mastery of the concepts and skills from the previous modules. The module will be used to introduce RP in daily life. This module will also introduce Harm Reduction and detail some applications of the Harm Reduction model.

Skills & Techniques

The module will be used to introduce RP in daily life by reviewing the distinction between lapses and relapse, high-risk situations, coping skills, and the continued (lifelong) use of the therapist and therapy techniques. Also in this module, the therapist will present the Abstinence Violation Effect (AVE). The AVE occurs when a client is in high-risk situation and views the potential lapse as so severe, that they may as well relapse. The client and therapist will practice identifying and coping with lapses.

Predicting and planning for lapses allows the client an opportunity to implement his plan, and avoid going down relapse AVE

Harm Reduction

Harm Reduction recognizes that the client is likely to lapse and possible relapse. It may be unrealistic to expect a total cessation of the behavior. Orienting towards harm reduction stance often works to prevent the AVE, and keep the client engaged in treatment. The drawback to this approach is the apparent endorsement of future offending. Nothing could be further from the truth. HR recognizes the possibility of lapses and attempts to remove their power by encouraging the planning for and mitigation of their consequences.

One element of Harm Reduction can be tied into the information gained from the functional assessment described earlier in this work. This was described differently earlier in this work under the positive addictions and lifestyle balance module. In the example of Lucas, the sexual harassment was a problematic manifestation of a fetish. Harm Reduction would direct the client to attempt to have this need met elsewhere, such that the severity of the impact on the workplace would be minimized. This could be done through having the client seek fetish-related activity outside the workplace. An example might be the encouragement of use of lingerie catalogs as stimulus materials at home, to develop what the behaviorists call stimulus control. The goal would to inform the client that the fetish is acceptable and understandable, and that should it occur, it would best for all if it occurred in the privacy of the client's home.

Lifestyle Balance & Positive Addiction Reminder

Lifestyle balance and positive addiction speak towards a similar need as that described in the harm reduction section. Harm Reduction identifies some elements of the sexual function of the behavior and recognizes the benefit of having these needs meet legally and outside the workplace. Lifestyle Balance and Positive Addiction work similarly, in that they encourage the client to have the functional elements of the inappropriate behavior met elsewhere. For example, if the harassment functions as a stress reliever, exercise and meditation may be encouraged. If titillation is the primary motive, as a transitory intervention, making use sexually explicit materials or attending nude dancing establishments may best serve the client. And of course, should a primary motivating factor be related to relationship difficulties with their partner, couples therapy, including possibly sex therapy, might be a great benefit.

Relapse Prevention Plan

The major homework element for this section is the refinement of the Relapse Prevention Plan. The clinician role in this effort to assist the client in developing a wieldy, useful, helpful, accurate, and comprehensive plan that details problems, both specifically and thematically, and outlines interventions at each stage both at the level of specifics and principles. Thus far, the client should have identified and been implementing strategies relating to lapse, relapse, SIDs, high-risk situations and outcome expectancies. The focus of this section is reviewing the plan comprehensively.

The specifics in this plan may be as simple as "leave the area," "journal it," and "contact therapist/support person." While the generals may be something akin to, "identify elements in this situation which cued your recognition of this as a high risk situation, and what elements you overlooked."

This module requires 2 sessions. In 2nd session, content should address the AVE, high-risk situations, and coping skills for high-risk situations.

Homework

Week one

- Modify the Relapse Prevention plan (use Relapse Prevention Plan Worksheet)

Schedule

15% Review
- Go over last week's homework—Decision Matrices
- Praise client for successful completion of Outcome Expectancies and Problem of Immediate Gratification Module
- Review SIDs, coping skills

10% Introduce Relapse Prevention in Daily Life
- Review Terms
  - Lapse, Relapse
  - High-Risk situations
- Answer any questions

50% Discuss Module
- Discuss Abstinence Violation Effect
- Practice lapse and relapse situations, give alternative beliefs and build skills
- Discuss continued use of therapy and have the client report those elements of therapy have "stuck" and are being practiced in daily living

25% Review
- Review progress made during session
- Outline next session's content and procedure

- Improve social supports in Relapse Prevention plan
- Identify possible environmental (workplace) interventions
- Implement and journal about Relapse Prevention plan

Week two

- Develop aftercare plan
- Modify Relapse Prevention plan to include environmental interventions and social supports
- Continue to implement Relapse Prevention plan in daily living
- Journal daily about implementation of Relapse Prevention plan

Repeat or proceed decision tree

The client is ready to proceed when they have

1) A relapse prevention plan
2) Identified high-risk situations, and skills for negotiating these situations
3) A commitment to aftercare

Useful Metaphors

The Captain

A boat captain needs many skills. Chief of these are an ability to pilot a ship safely though difficult passages, which entails recognizes those passages, and steering safely though. The captain also needs the ability to ensure that if an accident occurs, that at least the captain doesn't make things worse. The captain also needs skills in recovering from accidents, repairing the hull if there's been a crash, etc. The client is the captain, and their life is the ocean. The must negotiate through, and there is no final destination. They will be piloting their ship for the rest of their life.

"Buffy the Vampire Slayer"™

This popular television program details the life and troubles of a young vampire slayer. Her job is to fight the demons that are ever-present in her life, by making use of her training, skills, and support group. She usually, but not always, wins. Sometimes the vampires get a bite or two in before succumbing to her. As of the first printing of this manual, she has died twice, a useful comparison the likelihood of lapse (vampire bites and injuries) and relapsing (being killed). It happens, and it happens to the best. Fortunately for Buffy, the writers have managed to bring her back from the dead. For our clients, they need to know that even if they relapse, there is a chance for continued recovery. The client needs to know that lapses, and even relapses are to be expected, and the battle will continue as long as they live. Unfortunately for Buffy, as well as the client, there may be no vacation.

Sisyphus

The greedy king of Corinth, who in Greek mythology was sentenced to perpetually push the stone up the mountain. When he completed his task of pushing the boulder to the top of the mountain, it would roll to the bottom and he would start anew. The client's experience will be the same. For the rest of their life, they will need to see their boulder, and work on pushing their boulder uphill. Sometimes will be easier than others, and others will be less difficult, and if they stumble and it rolls to the bottom, they will need to start anew.

Therapy Transcript

T We're getting near the end of the road in our work together.

R So I'm free to go?

T Not just yet. A couple of things first. I need to see that you can take the book learning we've been doing and put it into place in the real world. And after that, we need to have a plan for when you leave.

R Ok, the second part sounds easier than the first part. I'm not too sure how to do the first part, other than have you look and see that I've not done anything to get in trouble since we've started.

T Good point, problem is, this is what I would call an artificial environment. When you're done, you're not going to have the weekly accountability that seeing me presents. You've got some extra incentives in place to 'behave' if that's the best word.

R Gotcha. And without you around to keep me in check, what are we to do?

T The first step is something you're already doing. Like you've said, you're living and going to work, and having opportunities to harass, and you're not doing that. What we need is your plan for how to manage those situations, and setting up what we'll call aftercare.

R Sounds good, like planned follow-ups after you go to the doctor.

T That's right, I want to see if this medicine takes.

R Makes sense. What's first?

T Before we get too far along with that, there's another element of treatment that's a common problem for people dealing with issues like the one we're working on here.

R So, we've got the PIG, and we've SIDs, I'm guessing this has three-letter acronym.

T Yup, the AVE, like in the Avenue to Relapse.

R A V E?

T Yah, want the definition first, or an example?

R Definition, and we'll see if I can come up with the example.

T All right, A V E is the Abstinence Violation Effect. Defined as when the terms of the behavior cessation program have been violated, leading to a return to pre-treatment levels of malfunctioning.

R So this would be the 'what the hell' thing.

T Tell me more.

R Like, say I was a drinker and I had a beer on my way home. What the hell, may as well finish the case.

T I think you've got it. Now, apply it to you.

R Ok, well... if I had a chance to lapse

T Right, not a relapse, the AVE leads to relapse, but you can save from a lapse

R Yah, so I'm lapsing, I've got a woman at her workstation, and I'm under the desk, and I rub her leg while I'm down there. The AVE would be when I grab her thigh on the way to up to have my balance, or cop a feel when I stumble.

T I think you're getting the hang of this. Now, I want you to play therapist for a while. Why is this an important element to put on the table?

R Well, like you said, it sounds like it could be a common problem. Especially if there's this all-or-nothing mindset. Like if I think there's only two ways of being, either has a harasser or as a non-harasser, that doesn't leave any fudge factor, or gray area.

T Ok, give me more...

R Ok, so if I'm in this all-or-none mindset, and I've violated the none aspect, that just leaves me with the all. Since I've violated the 'no' harassment, it's like; it's like giving me permission to have the 'all' harassment. And that's just totally screwing myself.

T Well said. And Like I said, it's a very common problem this all-or-none element that leads easily down the path to relapse—the AVE to relapse.

R Relapse AVE, I think I can remember that.

T Is Relapse AVE a one-way street?

R No, coz you don't have to go all the way down.

T What do you mean?

R I mean, I could stop along the way. Like if I'm a drinker, I could stop after one sip, one beer, one six-pack, one case, you know, like that, I could reduce the harm.

T Again, turn it towards you and your situation.

R All right, I could stop with the going under the desk, I could stop with the looking up her legs, I could stop at touching her, I could stop between touching her and a more forceful grab beyond a rub, I could stop anywhere in there. And I could also stop by skipping the porn as substitute, and I could stop by even if I, uhm, like even if I did a full blown escapade and harassed one, I could report myself so I didn't do it again later in the day or something like that.

T Now you're getting the hang of it. What else do you need to do?

R Dunno ... what are you looking for here?

T Well, let me give some hints—I'm thinking about the lifelong nature of this process ... like the metaphor I used earlier of Sisyphus.

R Oh, right. Ok, so I've lapsed and headed towards relapse. I've got to check my plan.

T What's the plan say?

R Call therapist, use the plan. Avoid the AVE

T Ok, so let's say you've called me—what are you going to say?

R I'm going to report that I've lapsed, that I've relapsed. That I need some booster sessions.

T Right on. What else have you got in the plan?

R That I need to call my old roommate from college. He got into some trouble like this before, and he didn't have the chance that I did to get treatment.

T Ok so far, what about the AVE?

R That I need to 'replace the thoughts'

T What do you have down for replacements?

R Here's one: My therapist and myself expected relapse. We also expect continued recovery.

T What else?

R It's not as bas as it seems right now. There's a chance for improvement?

T Sounds good so far, but it needs more...

MODULE 11: REVIEW AND AFTERCARE

Focus

The last module will be used to provide information about behavior in and out of the workplace. One of the essential elements of RP is the role of misbehavior in the context of one's life. This module is designed to assist the harasser in applying the lessons of the previous module to all aspects of their life. While the goal is the prevention of sexually harassing behaviors, the lifestyle will be addressed.

Skills & Techniques

The repairing of a damaged boat hull is an appropriate analogy. Patching the hole is well and good (reducing sexual harassment), but the pilot of the boat should also learn not to run the ship aground, through rapids or into icebergs (lifestyle balance). The development of positive addictions will be reviewed (Thompson, 1989). Positive addictions are healthy behaviors and hobbies, such as reading and bowling, in which the client can engage without experiencing adverse consequences. Thus, this module will serve as a capstone to integrate the material from the sexual harassment modules, in terms of the RP module.

The last module will serve as a review of each of the modules in isolation, and then as an integrated whole. For example, the harasser will review the role of myth acceptance as a component involved in sexual harassment, and then relate to how myth acceptance is involved in the RP model. This module will also allow time for planning and a review of problem solving strategies.

The last section of the eleventh module will be to address a plan for aftercare. How will the client handle situations in which they feel at risk for harassing? The client's support group will be outlined, and the therapist will work with the client to devise strategies for seeking help should the need arise. For example, the client and therapist will role-play situations in which the client will need to: ask a friend or loved one for help, call a therapist for an appointment, and tell a new friend about their history of sexual harassment and what the new friend can do to help the client when the client is in need.

Useful Metaphors

"Close a Door, Open a Window"

The thrust of this saying is that when we tell the client to 'stop' they need something to do instead. It is important to highlight the replacement behaviors that have been taught A common parenting example is when the small child misbehaves by playing with an inappropriate item, e.g., blender, the parent should encourage the interest in playing, and direct the child towards a more appropriate toy, e.g., ball. If the client is a parent, the applications of this aphorism in their life may cue their alternatives behaviors in daily living.

"Teach a Man to Fish..."

Another example taken from the Bible is the saying of 'give a man a fish, he eats for a meal, teach a man to fish, and he eats for life.' This

Schedule	
20%	Review Go over last week's homework Review successful and unsuccessful attempts at employing coping skills Praise client for successful completion of Relapse Prevention Plan
20%	Introduce Termination and Aftercare Explain procedure Answer any questions
60%	Review each module in isolation and as integrated whole Assessment, Overcoming Denial and Minimization, Skills Training, Myth Acceptance/Cognitive Distortions/Negative Attitudes Towards Women, Victim Empathy, SIDs and Coping Skills High-Risk Situations, Outcome Expectancies/PIG, RP in daily life.

aphorism highlights the abstraction of the rules taught in relapse prevention. RP is not a set of rules and if A, then B command rules. Rather, it is a set of principles related to the recognition of problematic situations and the appropriate response to these situations. RP, like fishing, is a general skill set to be taught, such that in novel situations, the client can rely on the training to inform the new predicament.

Life as a Terminal Condition

In service of orienting the client to the lifelong commitment of relapse prevention, it may be of benefit to liken life to a fatal disease. You beat the fatal disease when you die. Relapse prevention is like that, the graduation diploma for relapse prevention is usually one inch by three inches, and is affixed by a band to the big toe, and is awarded to people existing at room temperature. The purpose of placing RP in this context is orient the client to the long-term needs for follow-up and continued aftercare.

Homework

- Role-play successful coping skills
- Write detailed plan for aftercare
- Make use of a journal about use of functional support network
- Calls to therapist if unable to employ coping skills
- Continued implementation and modification of Relapse Prevention plan
- Any agenda items left from termination criteria listed below

Repeat or proceed decision tree

Clients are ready for termination when they can:

1) Disclose all sexual harassment incidents, both on and off the record, without attempts at minimizations, victim blaming, or distortions
2) Demonstrate accurate perceptions, interpretations, response generation, enactment and evaluation in social situations
3) Demonstrate correct identification of sexual harassment myths as myths
4) Recognize cognitive distortions as they occur, and correct them
5) Demonstrate empathy for victims through written work
6) Identify SIDs in their experience

7) Demonstrate realistic outcome expectancies for
8) As part of a comprehensive Relapse Prevention Plan,

   a) Have field-tested strategies for altering SIDs as they occur
   b) Identify high-risk situations
   c) Have field-tested an implementable strategies for negotiating high-risk situations
   d) Have a plan for addressing lapses and relapse for when they occur
   e) Have an aftercare program

Therapy Transcript

T Looks like we're close to wrapping this up.

R Yah, it's been a good run, and no offense, but it'll be nice to not be seeing you every week.

T No offense taken.

R So what's left?

T Well, I need to check in on a few things. First and foremost is your relapse prevention plan.

R I've got that here.

T Let's see it.

R Ok, here it is (hands over three ring binder)

T Quite a work, but from a guy who reads tech manuals, I think I expected this. How about if you walk me through it.

R Ok, first off is the cover page. This is the, if there was a fire and I needed to take one piece of paper with me, the back pocket plan, this is it.

T What's on it.

R Ok, well, it's got your number, the HR contacts number, and the number to the Crisis Line. And it's also got my mom's number on it. When we did the empathy thing, it really hit me how it world impact her if someone did this to her, so I've got her down there as a reminder.

T Cool—and like I said, there's going to things like that that I couldn't have predicted based on what we talked about, so I'm glad that you're really personalized this from the examples we've discussed.

R Ok, and it also has a quick definition of lapse, and relapse, and PIG, and AVE, and some of the other things, like my high-risk situations and examples of my SIDs. For example, here's one cool page-

T What's this?

R Well, it's sort of like that, objects in mirror are closer than they appear thing on the rearview mirror- this my you know you're in trouble ifs

T Like, you might be a redneck if…

R Yah, this, actually I've got this posted at my work station in a spot where I can see it,

T So what are they?

R I might be in trouble if I, 1) arrange to meet with a female coworker when I'm feeling stressed, 2) work later in the day, or in an isolated area, 3) work with a temp, especially if she's young and attractive, 4) work under the desk while she's there, 5) work over her shoulder, 6) I'm having troubles at home

T Sounds good.

R And I've also got my SIDs.

T Let's hear the SIDs.

R Ok, my SIDs list: My SIDs are anything I do that sets up some of the trouble spots on the other list. SIDs I have done before 1) check email or web to stall for time so a task waits until the end of the day, 2) promise one staff that I'll work on their problem first, so other problems have to wait until later in the day, 3) get dirty early in the day, so there are no qualms about spelunking later in the day, 4) putting off talking to my wife, so I'll have my bad day later in the day, 5) sending my assistant on a chore so I'll be alone later, I've done that one each time I've gotten busted, er, each time I harassed.

T Nice save.

R I've done a good bit of work on this.

T I can tell. Let's review some of the other checkpoints.

R Well, there's some of the template that you gave me that seem to fit, and some that don't. For example the chemical dependency stuff—that's drugs and alcohol, right?

T Right.

R Well, I don't drink much or do drugs, so I just put that if I started doing those things, that in and of itself would be enough to set of warning bells.

T Sounds good—what else?

R Well, the spirituality. That really got me thinking.

T Tell me more.

R Well, I've not been thinking much about God and stuff, but more about me being faithful to myself. Like, my spirituality is mostly within myself, I don't go to church or anything, but my spirituality is a lot about me being the person I want to be, and the person I present to the world. I feel spiritual when I'm being the kind of person I aspire to be.

T And when you're not?

R When I'm not I feel awful—which is part of what led to me coming in here. I mean I could have said, screw it—and taken a job somewhere else. But I wasn't being true to me.

T So how does the spirituality fit in?

R Here's how: If I'm not living in accord with my values, my personal mission statement, then I'm disrespecting myself. And that's not what my being spiritual is about. It's not like a big Christian thing or anything, but if I'm not being true to myself, it sees like I'm out of sorts with the way things out to be.

T I think I follow you, so for you, it wasn't about finding your inner Buddha, or turning to the Bible, but honoring yourself.

R Right, and I can see that I wasn't doing that. So in the spirituality section, I address that, about how to see what I want to be about, and do I want to be known as "the guy who cops a feel" or do I want to be the guy who respected others and himself, and was a go-to guy when there were problems.

T Sounds like this had a strong impact on you ...

Empirical Support of Intervention

We want to be sure of two things when administering psychotherapy. First, we want to minimize any risks of harm, and second, we want to only use treatments and interventions with demonstrated effectiveness. For treatments still in development, such as the one we propose, psychotherapists are morally and ethically obligated to frequently assess the impact of their intervention. Using a multiple baseline approach to guide the systematic collection of data can do that.

The multiple baseline approach can be quite similar to when you have a loose thread, and your pull on it. What happens? Sometimes the string pulls away from the garment, and other times, it pulls those threads next to it. For example, consider a fabric that has separate threads of victim empathy, outcome expectancies, cognitive distortions and myth acceptance. The modules of the treatment plan are intended to pull on one of these threads, victim empathy for example. When we introduce this module, and the client 'gets it' we expect to see an increase in victim empathy, but we don't expect to see strong movement in other areas, such as outcome expectancies. The multiple baseline approach allows you to pull the threads one at a time, and observe the effects on your outcome measures, such as those described in the assessment section. Please refer to Hayes, Barlow, and Nelson-Gray, (1999), *The Scientist-Practitioner: Research and Accountability in the Age of Managed Care* for more on the opportunities and methodologies available for practitioner research.

Conclusion

The negative consequences of sexual harassment can be quite damaging for all parties involved. Unfortunately, the usual remedies are transferring the harasser, firing the harasser, or recommending that cure-all, "psychotherapy." And while "psychotherapy" has a general practice has been beneficial in some cases, we've also seen at treatments and interventions designed for a specific problem have demonstrated their effectiveness, for example, the bell and pad for enuresis, Barlow's treatment for panic, and Linehan's Dialectical Behavior Therapy for parasuicidal individuals. Thus, the development a relapse-prevention based treatment specific for the problem of sexual harassers. This treatment has 11 content modules designed to impact the key motivating factors for sexual harassment.

References

Bandura, A. (1977). *Social learning theory*. Englewood Cliffs, NJ: Prentice Hall.

Bell, A. & Rollnick, S. (1996). Motivational interviewing in practice: A structured approach. In F. Rotgers & D. Keller (Eds.) *Treating substance abuse: Theory and Technique*. New York: Guilford.

Burns, S. E. (1995). Issues in workplace sexual harassment law and related social science research. *Journal of Social Issues, 51*, 193–207.

Conte, A. (1997). Legal theories of sexual harassment. In W. T. O'Donohue (Ed.) *Sexual Harassment: Theory, research, and treatment*. Needham Heights, MA: Allyn & Bacon.

Dansky, B. S. & Kilpatrick, D. G. (1997). Effects of sexual harassment. In W. T. O'Donohue (Ed.) *Sexual Harassment: Theory, research, and treatment* Needham Heights, MA: Allyn & Bacon.

Dobson, K. S. & Shaw, B. F. (1988). The use of treatment manuals in cognitive therapy: Experience and issues. *Journal of Consulting and Clinical Psychology, 56*, 673–680.

Fitzgerald, L. F., Swan, S., & Magley, V. J. (1997). But was it really sexual harassment? Legal, behavioral, and psychological definitions of the workplace victimization of women. In W. T. O'Donohue (Ed.) *Sexual Harassment: Theory, research, and treatment*. Needham Heights, MA: Allyn & Bacon.

Fultz, J., Schaller, M., & Cialdini, R. (1988). Empathy, sadness, and distress: Three related but distinct vicarious affective responses to another's suffering. *Personality and Social Psychology Bulletin, 14*, 312–325.

Gambrill, E. (1995a). Assertion skills training. In W. T. O'Donohue & Krasner, L. (Eds.) Handbook of psychological skills training: Clinical techniques and applications (pp. 81–118). Needham Heights, MA: Allyn & Bacon.

Gambrill, E. (1995b). Helping shy, socially anxious, and lonely adults: A skill-based contextual approach. In W. T. O'Donohue & Krasner, L. (Eds.) *Handbook of psychological skills training: Clinical techniques and applications* (pp. 247–286). Needham Heights, MA: Allyn & Bacon.

Gosselin, H. L. (1986). Sexual harassment on the job: Psychological, social and economic repercussions. *Canadian Mental Health, 32*, 21–24.

Gruber, J. E. (1990). Methodological problems and policy implications in sexual harassment research. *Population Research and Policy Review, 9*, 235–254.

Gruber, J. E. (1997). An epidemiology of sexual harassment: Evidence from North American and Europe. In W. T. O'Donohue (Ed.) *Sexual harassment: Theory, research, and treatment*. Needham Heights, MA: Allyn & Bacon.

Grundman, E. O., O'Donohue, W. T. & Peterson, S. H. (1997). The prevention of sexual harassment. In W. T. O'Donohue (Ed.) *Sexual Harassment: Theory, research, and treatment*. Needham Heights, MA: Allyn & Bacon.

Hall, G. C. N. (1995). The preliminary development of theory-based community treatment for sexual offenders. *Professional Psychology: Research and Practice, 26*, 478–483.

Hayes, S. C., Barlow, D. H., & Nelson-Gray, R. O. (1999). *The scientist-practitioner: Research and accountability in the age of managed care.* Needham Heights MA: Prentice Hall (Allyn & Bacon).

Hayes, S. C., Strosahl, K. D., & Wilson, K. G. (1999). *Acceptance and commitment therapy: An experiential approach to behavior change.* New York: Guilford Press.

Heather, N., Rollnick, S., Bell, A., & Richmond, R. (1996). Effects of brief counseling among male heavy drinkers identified on general hospital wards. *Drug and Alcohol Review, 15,* 29–38.

Jenkins-Hall, K. D. (1989). Cognitive restructuring. In D. R. Laws (Ed.) *Relapse prevention with sex offenders.* New York: Guilford.

Jenkins-Hall, K. D. & Marlatt, G. A. (1989). Apparently irrelevant decisions in the relapse process. In D. R. Laws (Ed.) *Relapse prevention with sex offenders.* New York: Guilford.

Jones, T. S. & Remland, M. S. (1992). Sources of variability in perceptions of and responses to sexual harassment. *Sex Roles, 27,* 121–142.

Kohlenberg, R. J. & Tsai, M. (1991). *Functional analytic psychotherapy: Creating intense and curative therapeutic relationships.* New York: Kluwer Academic/Plenum Publishers.

Laws, D. R. (Ed.) (1989). *Relapse prevention with sex offenders.* New York: Guilford.

Laws, D. R. (1995). A theory of relapse prevention. In W. T. O'Donohue, & Krasner, L. (Eds.) *Theories of behavior therapy: Exploring behavior change.* Washington DC: American Psychological Association.

Laws, D. R. (1997). *The harm reduction alternative to relapse Prevention.* Paper presented at the 16th Annual meeting of the Association for the Treatment of Sexual Abusers, Arlington, Virginia.

Laws, D. R. & O'Donohue, W. (1997). Introduction. In D. R. Laws & O'Donohue, W. (Eds.) *Sexual deviance.* New York: Guilford.

Laws, D. R., Hudson, S. M., & Ward, T. (Eds.) (2000). *Remaking relapse prevention with sexual offenders: A sourcebook.* Thousand Oaks CA: Sage.

Linehan, M. M. (1993). *Cognitive-behavioral treatment of borderline personality disorder.* New York: Guilford.

MacDonald, R. K. & Pithers, W. D. (1989). Self-monitoring to identify high-risk situations. In D. R. Laws (Ed). *Relapse prevention with sex offenders.* New York: Guilford.

Malamuth, N. M. (1986). Predictors of naturalistic sexual aggression. *Journal of Personality and Social Psychology, 50,* 953–962.

Maletzky, B. M. (1997). Exhibitionism: Assessment and treatment. In D. R. Laws & O'Donohue, W. T. (Eds.) *Sexual Deviance.* New York: Guilford.

Marlatt, G. A. (1989). Feeding the PIG: The problem of immediate gratification. In D. R. Laws (Ed.) *Relapse prevention with sex offenders.* New York: Guilford.

Marlatt, G. A. & Gordon, J. R. (1980). Determinants of relapse: Implications for the maintenance of behavior change. *British Journal of Addiction, 79,* 261–273.

Marques, J. K. & Nelson, C. (1989). Elements of high-risk situations for sex offenders. In D. R. Laws (Ed). *Relapse prevention with sex offenders.* New York: Guilford.

McDonel, E. C. & McFall, R. M. (1991). Construct validity of two heterosexual perception skill measures for assessing rape proclivity. *Violence and Victims, 6,* 17–30.

McMullin, R. E. (1986). *Handbook of cognitive therapy techniques.* New York: Norton.

Miller, W. R. (1996). Motivational interviewing: Research, practice, and puzzles. *Addictive Behaviors, 21,* 835–842.

Nelson, C. & Jackson, P. (1989). High-risk recognition: The cognitive-behavioral chain. In D. R. Laws (Ed.) *Relapse prevention with sex offenders.* New York: Guilford.

O'Donohue, W. T. (1997). Introduction. In W. O'Donohue (Ed.) *Sexual harassment: Theory, research and practice.* Boston: Allyn & Bacon.

O'Donohue, W., Fitzgerald, L., & Brunswig, K. A. (1999). *A self-report sexual harassment inventory*. Paper presented at the 18th Annual Meeting of the Association for the Treatment of Sexual Abusers, Lake Buena Vista, Florida.

O'Donohue, W. T. & Letourneau, E. (1993). A brief group treatment for the modification of denial in child sexual abusers: Outcome and follow-up. *Child Abuse and Neglect, 17*, 299–304.

O'Donohue, W., Penix, T. M., & Brunswig, K. A. (under review). Development and Evaluation of a Sexual Harassment Sensitivity and Prevention Training Program: A Cognitive Approach.

Persons, J. B. (1989). *Cognitive therapy in practice: A case formulation approach*. New York: Norton.

Pithers, W. D., Beal, L. S., Armstrong, J., & Petty, J. (1989). Identification of risk factors through clinical interviews and analysis of risk factors. In D. R. Laws (Ed.) *Relapse prevention with sex offenders*. New York: Guilford.

Rabinowitz, V. C. (1990). Coping with sexual harassment. In M. Paludi (Ed.) Ivory power: *Sexual harassment on campus*. Albany, NY: SUNY Press.

Sandberg, G. G. & Marlatt, G. A. (1989). Relapse fantasies. In D. R. Laws (Ed.) *Relapse prevention with sex offenders*. New York: Guilford.

Steenman, H., Nelson C., & Viesti, C. Jr. (1989). Developing coping strategies for high-risk situations. In D. R. Laws (Ed.) *Relapse prevention with sex offenders*. New York: Guilford.

Thompson, J. K. (1989). Lifestyle interventions: Promoting positive addictions. In D. R. Laws (Ed.) *Relapse prevention with sex offenders*. New York: Guilford.

United States Merit Systems Protection Board (1981). *Sexual harassment of federal workers: Is it a problem?* Washington, DC: Government Printing Office.

United States Merit Systems Protection Board (1987). *Sexual harassment of federal workers: An update*. Washington, DC: Government Printing Office.

Wagner, E. J. (1992). *Sexual harassment in the workplace: How to prevent, investigate and resolve problems in your organization*. New York: AMACOM.

Handouts

The authors & publishers grant to individual purchasers of this text nonassignable permission to reproduce the handouts and homework sheets in this manual for clinical use with their clients.

- Handout #1 The FAQs of Sexual Harassment
- Handout #2 Motivation Ratings
- Handout #3 Self-Report Sexual Harassment Inventory
- Handout #4 Sexual Harassment Knowledge Questionnaire
- Handout #5 Sexual Harassment Myth Acceptance
- Handout #6 Empathy Worksheet
- Handout #7 Outcome Expectancies
- Handout #8 Cognitive Distortions
- Handout #9 Relapse Prevention Offense Chain Worksheet
- Handout #10 Relapse Prevention Plan Worksheet

The FAQs of Sexual Harassment

What it is
Three types of sexual harassment:

<u>Quid pro quo</u>
• Literally, this for that involves a trade or bargain of sexual activity for beneficial treatment

<u>Gender harassment</u>
• The creation of a hostile work environment based upon biological sex or gender
• Making disparaging comments about one gender; such as all men are pigs
• Display of erotic or explicit materials, such as pin-ups or beefcake posters
• A systematized or intuitional setting that fosters favoritism or denigration based upon gender or sexuality
• Introducing an unwanted sexual element to the workplace, such as asking for a date after being told it was not wanted

<u>3rd party harassment</u>
• Is a hybrid of quid pro quo and gender harassment
• Results when a person not involved in a quid pro quo arrangement is denied an equal opportunity for beneficial treatment, an example, Woman A receives a promotion based on quid pro quo arrangement, Woman B claims 3 rd party harassment as she was denied an opportunity to compete fairly for the promotion.

What is the policy?
• Generally company policy defers to legal standards

What is the law?
• Reasonable woman
• Reasonable person

For both of these standards, courts instruct the jury to weigh the behavior based on the standard of what a reasonable person/woman would find offensive. This results in some variability from jurisdiction to jurisdiction, and within juries.

• Intent doesn't matter

Courts often instruct juries that the intent of the alleged harasser does not matter; rather, the outcome of the interaction is the key element.

• Can be contact or non-contact

Sexual harassment can be hands-on as well as hands-off

• Can be civil as well as criminal

Sexual harassment can result in civil charges under Title IX

Sexual harassment can result in civil charges under assault, battery and sex crimes

• The "slut defense" will not work

Though often attempted, attacking a victim's history rarely sways juries

• Male-male, male-female, female-female and female-male harassment suits have been filed

Simply put, there is no safe-zone for sexual harassment

• That someone else has "gotten away with it" may not mitigate your responsibility

That someone else has not been reported won't change the impact of your behavior

What are the rules?

• Know the policy

• Know the law

• If you wouldn't do it in front of your partner or children or in church, you probably don't want to do it at work

What are the results?

• For you

You'll likely lose your job
With this on your resume, you'll likely be underemployed evermore
Public humiliation may be the result of media coverage
Spouse and children, neighbors and friends may not support you
You may feel guilt, anguish, sadness and depression, among others

• For your victim

They will likely feel uncomfortable at the workplace
They will be embarrassed an humiliated
They will feel victimized
They may feel guilt
They may feel shame
If they have a history of victimization, they may have memories of previous abuse
They may have difficulty in their relationships with loved ones
They will likely experience some of these symptoms

Depression
Anxiety
Intrusive images
Nightmares
Flashbacks
Sleep difficulties
Fear

Handout #2 Motivation Ratings

Indicate the certainty with which you would perform the following behaviors:

Very Certain							Uncertain
	1	2	3	4	5	6	7

I would not make negative comments regarding someone's gender

1 2 3 4 5 6 7

I would touch someone at work if I were sexually attracted to him or her

1 2 3 4 5 6 7

I would encourage my coworkers to use sexual attention or favors to get the job done

1 2 3 4 5 6 7

I would get consent before telling an off-color joke in the workplace

1 2 3 4 5 6 7

I would promote someone for sex

1 2 3 4 5 6 7

I would not comment on my coworker's appearance

1 2 3 4 5 6 7

I would ignore sexual behaviors in my place of business

1 2 3 4 5 6 7

I would characterize people who do not like sexual innuendo in the workplace as "uptight"

1 2 3 4 5 6 7

I would change my behavior in the workplace if I knew it was offensive to someone

1 2 3 4 5 6 7

I am motivated to decrease the likelihood that I will engage in unwelcome sexual behaviors in my workplace

1 2 3 4 5 6 7

Handout #3 Self-Report Sexual Harassment Inventory

Using this scale, please indicate how often you have done the following

0 = never
1 = once or twice
2 = more than twice
3 = often
4 = many times

1. Have you ever been in a work situation where you habitually told your coworkers or supervisees sexually suggestive stories or offensive jokes? ____

2. Have you ever been a situation where you made crude and offensive sexual remarks either publicly (for example in the office), or to your coworkers or supervisees? ____

3. Have you ever been a situation where you treated your coworkers or supervisees "differently" because of their gender (i.e. mistreated, slighted, or ignored them)? ____

4. Have you ever been a situation where you were condescending toward your coworkers or supervisees or "put them down" because of their gender? ____

5. Have you ever been in a situation where you displayed, used, or distributed sexist or sexually suggestive materials (e.g. pictures, stories, or pornography)? ____

6. Have you ever been a situation where you made sexist remarks (e.g. suggest that women are too emotional to be scientists or to assume leadership roles)? ____

7. Have you ever been in a situation where you made unwanted attempts to draw coworkers or supervisees into a discussion of personal or sexual matters (e.g. attempted to discuss or comment on your sex life)? ____

8. Have you ever been a situation where you gave coworkers or supervisees unwanted sexual attention? ____

9. Have you ever been a situation where you attempted to establish a romantic sexual relationship with a co-worker or supervisee despite their efforts to discourage you? ____

10. Have you ever been a situation where you have continued to ask a co-worker or supervisee for dates drinks, dinner, etc., even though they had said "no"? ____

11. Have you ever been a situation where you touched a coworker or supervisee (e.g. laid a hand on their bare arm, put an arm around their shoulders) in a way that made them feel uncomfortable? ____

12. Have you ever been a situation where you made unwanted attempts to stroke or fondle a coworker or supervisee (e.g. stroking their leg or neck, touching their breast, etc.)? ____

13. Have you ever been in a situation where you made unwanted attempts to have sex with a coworker or supervisee that resulted in their pleading or physically struggling? ____

14. Have you ever been a situation where you made a coworker or supervisee feel like they were being subtly bribed for some sort of reward or special treatment to engage in sexual behavior? ____

15. Have you ever been in a situation where you made a coworker or supervisee feel subtly threatened with some sort of retaliation for not being sexually cooperative (e.g. the mention of an upcoming evaluation, review, etc.)? _____

16. Have you ever been in a situation where you implied faster promotions or better treatment if a co-worker or supervisee was sexually cooperative? _____

17. Have you ever been in a situation where you made it necessary for a coworker or supervisee to respond positively to sexual or social invitations in order to be well treated on the job? _____

18. Have you ever been in a situation where you made a coworker or supervisee feel they would be treated poorly if they didn't cooperate sexually? _____

19. Have you ever been a situation where you treated a coworker or supervisee badly for refusing to have sex? _____

20. Have you ever sexually harassed a coworker, customer, or other woman in your workplace? _____

21. Has anyone ever said you sexually harassed anyone in your workplace? _____

Handout #4 Sexual Harassment Knowledge Questionnaire

True or False

1. Sexual harassment is defined as any unwanted sexual attention. ____
2. As long as you didn't mean to sexually harass a co-worker your behavior is not considered sexual harassment. ____
3. Sexual harassment is not a violation of a person's civil rights. ____
4. The law considers the intent of the person committing the sexually harassing action in determining if sexual harassment has occurred. ____
5. As long as you don't touch a woman, you can say things like "women don't make good managers," and not be committing any type of sexual harassment. ____
6. Sexual harassment is a violation of both civil and criminal law. ____
7. Telling dirty jokes at work is okay, and not considered sexual harassment. ____
8. Asking a woman to have sex with you in exchange for a raise or promotion is considered *quid pro quo* sexual harassment. ____
9. Rating a woman on a scale from 1 to 10 in front of other women would not be considered sexual harassment under the current laws. ____
10. Although sexual harassment is illegal, statements like, "If an equally qualified man and woman apply for a job, the man should get the job," are okay. ____
11. Statements like "men are stupid" are a form of sexual harassment called gender harassment. ____
12. Even if you sexually harass someone you can't be fired or demoted. ____
13. As long as you can prove a person was "asking for it" your actions cannot be considered sexual harassment. ____
14. If you can prove that your attention was wanted then your actions will not be considered sexual harassment in a court of law. ____
15. Gender harassment, for example, saying "women don't belong in the workplace" is not legally considered sexual harassment. ____
16. Repeatedly asking someone out for a date who has said no, could be considered sexual harassment. ____

17. Even though the law states that any unwanted sexual attention is illegal, there are some forms of unwanted sexual attention that are not considered sexual harassment. ____
18. The reasonable woman standard, which means that any behavior a reasonable woman would see as sexual harassment is sexual harassment, has been upheld in court. ____
19. As long as you don't see your actions as unwelcome then you are not engaging in sexually harassing behaviors. ____
20. Rubbing a woman's shoulders is not sexual harassment as long as you are just trying to keep work a friendly place. ____
21. Posting sexually explicit material in your office, such as "beefcake" posters is just harmless "girls' stuff" and not sexual harassment. ____
22. A man can be sexually harassed by a woman or another man. ____
23. As long as an offensive joke is sent via email, and not face-to-face, it is not sexual harassment. ____
24. Third party harassment, in which someone denied a promotion due to a *quid pro quo* arrangement between two others, has been considered sexual harassment in a court of law. ____
25. Even though he does not work for your company, the deliveryman can legally make claims of sexual harassment if he receives unwanted sexual attention while delivering a package to your workplace. ____
26. If you are found responsible for an act of sexual harassment, the company for whom you work bears sole financial responsibility for any lawsuit. ____
27. A woman cannot sexually harass another woman. ____
28. Spreading a little sexual gossip about a co-worker can be considered sexual harassment. ____
29. If your boss tells a risqué joke, you cannot be found to have sexually harassed if you tell the same joke to other coworkers. ____
30. Giving a coworker a supportive swat on the bottom is an appropriate form of encouragement. ____

Handout #5 Sexual Harassment Myth Acceptance

Please rate the following statements according to this scale:

Believe Strongly	Believe Some	Neutral	Generally disbelieve	Disbelieve strongly
1	2	3	4	5

1. If an equally qualified man and woman applied for a position, the man should get the job ____
2. All people like to be told they are sexy, even at work ____
3. People who have a "reputation" around the office don't care if you make sexually explicit jokes in their presence. ____
4. Women are less rational than men are ____
5. Men are more capable of hard work than women ____
6. If someone owes their job to their boss, the boss is right to expect sexual attention or favors in return ____
7. No one can be forced to have sex if they don't really want to ____
8. Women are better in the home while men are better in the workplace ____
9. Men should be strong and always ready for sex ____
10. People secretly enjoy being hit on at work ____
11. You have to do and return favors to move up in the world ____
12. Sexual harassment is just people trying to get money from coworkers or companies they don't like ____
13. Women are the only objects of sexual harassment ____
14. People who smile a lot want sexual attention ____
15. Work is a good place to find sexual partners ____
16. People have a right to decorate their work area in any way they choose, even with sexy pictures ____
17. Blowing off steam by flirting and telling jokes of a sexual nature is natural and expected ____
18. Gay men are the only ones who harass other men ____

19. Women are flattered by sexual advances from men even when they fail to positively respond to these advances ____
20. It is natural for men to be more aggressive when it comes to sexual relations with women ____
21. Women are often inconsistent in terms of their non-verbal communications with men ____
22. Women often mean "maybe" or even "yes" when they say "no" to sexual advances by men ____
23. It is important for men to control the initial development of their relationships with women ____
24. Women frequently use men to obtain status, security, or other things that they want ____
25. Women who dress in a sexy manner at work are deliberately ending a message to men ____
26. Highly attractive individuals (opposite sex for heterosexuals) "drive me crazy" and I sometimes do or say thing around them that I can't help ____
27. Pregnant women use their condition to justify doing less work on many jobs in comparison to their coworkers ____
28. Women are often flattered by sexual advances from their male coworkers ____

Handout #6 Empathy Worksheet

1. After the copy machine jammed again, with a deadline looming in front of you, you tell the female secretary that she is "just a stupid bitch who can't keep the damn copier running – why don't you just go back to the kitchen where you belong."

How does she feel about herself?

How does she feel about you?

How do you feel about yourself?

How do you feel about her?

Notes

2. You see two coworkers, to whom you attracted, talking and look ing in your direction. You see one of them point at you, then turn to the other, while holding her fingers slightly apart and laugh.

How do you feel about them?

How do you feel about yourself?

Notes

3. You and a buddy at work notice are commenting to each other about the physical attributes of the new temp. Just as you say, "she has a nice rack" the temp's supervisor walks behind you.

How does she feel about you?

How does the supervisor feel about you?

How do you feel about yourself?

How do you feel about your buddy?

How does your buddy feel about you?

How do you feel about her?

4. Continuing #3 above, the supervisor then walks to the temp, and speaks to her in hushed tones. You notice the temp blush, and quickly leave the work area.

How does she feel about you?

How does the supervisor feel about you?

How do you feel about yourself?

How do you feel about your buddy?

How does your buddy feel about you?

How do you feel about her?

5. You notice a coworker who seems to having a rough day. You walk over to this person and give her a shoulder rub. You feel her pull away from you. You tell her to "lighten up, you just need to relax."

How does she feel about herself?

How does she feel about you?

How do you feel about yourself?

How do you feel about her?

Notes

6. You have heard through the office grapevine that a coworker does not share your sexual orientation. When in conversation with this person, you make several innuendos about their orientation.

How does this person feel about himself or herself?

How does this person feel about you?

How do you feel about this person?

How do you feel about yourself?

Notes

Handout #7 Outcome Expectancies

Describe the Harassing Behavior or Situation: ______________________________

____

____

____

List the short-term positive consequences of harassing:

1.____

2.____

3.____

List the long-term positive consequences of harassing:

1.____

2.____

3.____

List the short-term negative consequences of harassing:

1.____

2.____

3.____

List the long-term negative consequences of harassing:

1.____

2.____

3.____

List the short-term positive consequences of <u>not</u> harassing:

1._____

2._____

3._____

List the long-term positive consequences of <u>not</u> harassing:

1._____

2._____

3._____

List the short-term negative consequences of <u>not</u> harassing:

1._____

2._____

3._____

List the long-term negative consequences of <u>not</u> harassing:

1._____

2._____

3._____

Handout #8

Common Cognitive Distortions – Stinking Thinking – Thinking Errors

Victim Blaming – She led me on...
Entitlement – I deserve to...
Minimizing – It's not as bad as they said, all I did was...
Rationalizing – All the guys do it, I was the one to be made example of...
Projection – The other person wanted what I wanted...
Magnification – She said she was interested in hearing about my new boat, and this shows that she was interested in me...
Victim stance – Here's another example of how they're out to make it tough for me...
Catastrophizing – I shouldn't even bother trying, there's no hope in me ever doing things differently...
Overgeneralizing – like catastrophizing and magnification, it's like the old saying goes – give an inch and they'll take a mile. Since she didn't report it the first time, she must not have minded any other time...
All-or-nothing – Like the above, seeing one's self in absolute terms leads one to be easily criticized or devalued and supports the abstinence violation effect
Negative bias – Unrealistic perception of all events as negative, e.g., Even though I was complimented on my presentation, they didn't say anything nice about me...
Positive bias - Unrealistic perception of events as positive, e.g., Even though he said my presentation needed some more polish, if that's the worst he could come up with, he must think it was fantastic...
Personalization – inferring a personal meaning to non-personal events, e.g., She liked my presentation, so she must like me...

For each of the cognitive errors listed below, answer the following questions
1) Is this a problem for me?
2) What does this look like when I do it?
3) What the most recent example of this cognitive error
4) How many times have I done this in the last seven days?

Victim Stance
1)____
2)____
3)____
4)____
Entitlement
1)____
2)____
3)____
4)____
Minimizing
1)____
2)____
3)____
4)____

Rationalizing
1)__________
2)__________
3)__________
4)__________

Projection
1)__________
2)__________
3)__________
4)__________

Magnification
1)__________
2)__________
3)__________
4)__________

Victim Stance
1)__________
2)__________
3)__________
4)__________

Catastrophizing
1)__________
2)__________
3)__________
4)__________

Over generalizing
1)__________
2)__________
3)__________
4)__________

All-or-nothing
1)__________
2)__________
3)__________
4)__________

Negative Bias
1)__________
2)__________
3)__________
4)__________

Positive Bias
1)__________
2)__________
3)__________
4)__________

Personalization
1)__________
2)__________
3)__________
4)__________

My Relapse Prevention Plan

Offense Chain Worksheet

When completing this worksheet, you may be directed to describe a single event that led to your participation in this intervention, your most recent event, a typical event, or the general theme across all instances of your sexually inappropriate behavior

I. Setting the Stage – where are you, what are you doing, how do you feel?

____

____

____

____

____

II. Seemingly Unimportant Decisions (SIDs)

Seemingly Irrelevant/Unimportant Decisions (SIDS/SUDS): Decisions early in a behavior chain that place the client in a high-risk situation, e.g., the drinker deciding to get milk from the market near the liquor store rather than the market near day care center.

____

____

____

____

____

III. Risky Situation

High Risk Situation: A situation identified by client and therapist as one in which the client has a greater likelihood to experience a lapse or relapse. Part of a behavior chain that probabilistically could lead to a lapse or relapse.

IV. Lapse

Lapse: An occurrence of an undesired behavior in the context of behavior cessation or reduction program (e.g., smoking a cigarette by the client in a smoking cessation program or visiting a bar by an alcoholic). A lapse is always less serious than a relapse.

V. Abstinence Violation Effect (AVE)

Abstinence Violation Effect (AVE): The AVE occurs when a client lapses and irrationally concludes that the lapse is so severe, that they may as well relapse (e.g., since I broke the rule and I had one shot of whiskey, I may as well finish the bottle); a form of perfectionist or "all or none" thinking.

VI. Relapse

Relapse: A violation of the contract or terms of the behavior cessation or reduction program. Sometimes defined as a return to pretreatment levels of the problem behavior.

Notes

My Relapse Prevention Plan

Worksheet

Emergency Numbers

Therapist ______________________________

Peer Support ______________________________

____

____

Human Resources Contact ______________________________

____

____

Definitions:

What my lapses look like ______________________________

____

____

What my relapses look like ______________________________

____

____

What to do when I lapse (or recognize that I've lapsed) ______________________________

____

____

____

What to do when I relapse (or recognize that I've relapsed) ______________________________

____

____

____

My Relapse Prevention Plan

Worksheet

What PIG means to mean ______________________________

____

____

What are my SIDs ______________________________

____

____

What are my High Risk Situations ______________________________

____

____

What sets my stage ______________________________

____

____

What are my cognitive distortions ______________________________

____

____

What does my AVE look like? ______________________________

____

____

Other Issues

Chemical Dependency ______________________________

Comorbid concerns

Anxiety ______________________________

Depression ______________________________

Personality Disorder ______________________________

My Relationship ______________________________

My Spirituality ______________________________

How tos:

1) How to avoid High Risk Situations/lapse/relapse ______________________

2) How to cope in High Risk Situations/lapse/relapse ______________________

3) How to escape High Risk Situations/lapse/relapse ______________________

4) How to re-group after a High Risk Situation/lapse/relapse ______________________

Index

About the Authors

KIRK A. BRUNSWIG works as a Team Leader for a civil commitment program for those adjudicated to be sexually violent predators. At this facility, Mr. Brunswig works primarily with the special needs subset of this population. Mr. Brunswig is also an advanced doctoral student in the clinical psychology program at the University of Nevada, Reno. Mr. Brunswig earned a M. S. at Western Washington University with a concentration in Measurement, Evaluation, and Statistical Analysis while he earned his B. S., *summa*, at Washington State University.

Kirk Brunswig has authored recent publications on Relapse Prevention and Sexual Harassment. He has also made several presentations at both national and international conferences in the field of sexual harassment. Most recently, Mr. Brunswig has chaired a symposium outlining the benefits of viewing sexual harassment as sexual abuse. Mr. Brunswig has also served as a conference discussant and paper presenter in sharing his research. Mr. Brunswig and Dr. O'Donohue have presented a workshop on the treatment of sexually harassing clients using a Relapse Prevention Model.

Kirk Brunswig has taught several undergraduate courses in psychology, including Abnormal Psychology, Psychological Assessment, and Statistical Methods.

WILLIAM O'DONOHUE is the Nicholas Cummings Professor of Organized Behavioral Health Care Delivery at the University of Nevada, Reno. Dr. O'Donohue is a full professor in the clinical psychology program at the University of Nevada, Reno, and an adjunct professor in both the Department of Psychiatry and the Department of Philosophy. Dr. O'Donohue earned his Ph. D. in clinical psychology at the State University of New York, Stony Brook. Dr. O'Donohue also has a Master's degree in Philosophy from Indiana University.

William O'Donohue, a licensed clinical psychologist, has published an extensive body of work on sexual deviance and sexual harassment. Most notably, Dr. O'Donohue recently edited the authoritative text, *Sexual Harassment: Research, Theory and Treatment* (1997: Allyn & Bacon). Along with D. Richard Laws, he was the co-editor of *Sexual Deviance: Theory, Assessment and Treatment* (1997: Guilford Press). He has served as an expert witness concerning many aspects of sexual harassment for both defendants and plaintiffs. Dr. O'Donohue was recently awarded a research grant from the National Institute of Mental Health to design, produce, and evaluate a sexual harassment prevention program. The outcome data concerning this program indicate that it is uniquely effective in a) educating employees about sexual harassment; b) producing psychological change on key attitudes that result in a decrease in the motivation to sexually harass; and c) imparting a sense of responsibility.

44184124R00095

Made in the USA
Middletown, DE
30 May 2017